Something About Home

New Writing on Migration and Belonging

Edited by

LIAM HARTE

GEOGRAPHY PUBLICATIONS

First published in 2017
by Geography Publications, Kennington Road, Templeogue, Dublin 6W
http://www.geographypublications.com/
with the assistance of the
UK Arts and Humanities Research Council

ISBN 978 0906602 843

Design and typesetting by Keystrokes Digital, Dublin
Printed by Grehan Printers, Dublin

Contents

II
'The crystal clear air and stillness of west Mayo…'

III
'On my Manchester moon...'

Contributors

The Editor

Liam Harte was born and raised in County Mayo and educated at NUI Galway and Trinity College Dublin. He is now Senior Lecturer in Irish and Modern Literature at the University of Manchester. He is the author or editor of eight books, the most recent of which is *Reading the Contemporary Irish Novel 1987-2007* (Wiley-Blackwell, 2014). His next book, *A History of Irish Autobiography*, is forthcoming from Cambridge University Press.

The Workshop Leaders

Moyra Donaldson is an award-winning poet and an experienced creative writing facilitator from County Down. She has published six collections of poetry, most recently *Selected Poems* (2012) and *The Goose Tree* (2014), both from Liberties Press in Dublin. Other collections include *Snakeskin Stilettos* (1998), *Beneath the Ice* (2001) and *The Horse's Nest* (2006), all published by Lagan Press in Belfast. Moyra is also widely published in magazines, journals and anthologies in both Europe and the USA. Her latest project was a collaboration with photographic artist Victoria J Dean, resulting in an exhibition and the publication *Abridged 0 — 36: Dis-Ease*. Website: moyradonaldson.blogspot.com

John McAuliffe is a distinguished Irish poet who has lived and worked in England since 2002. His fourth book, *The Way In* (2015), which was joint winner of the 2016 Michael Hartnett Poetry Award, is published by Gallery Press, as were *Of All Places* (2011), which was a PBS Recommendation, *Next Door* (2007) and *A Better Life* (2002), which was shortlisted for a Forward prize. He directs the Centre for New Writing at the University of Manchester, where he teaches poetry and edits *The Manchester Review*. He also writes a monthly poetry column for the *Irish Times*.

Mike McCormack is the author of two collections of short stories, *Getting It in the Head* (1996) and *Forensic Songs* (2012), and three novels, *Crowe's Requiem* (1998), *Notes from a Coma* (2005) and *Solar Bones* (2016). In 1996 he was awarded the Rooney Prize for Literature and *Getting It in the Head* was chosen as a *New York Times* Notable Book of the Year. A short film, which he scripted from one of the stories in that collection, was longlisted for an Academy Award in 2003. In 2006

Notes from a Coma was shortlisted for the Irish Book of the Year Award; it was published by Soho Press in New York in 2013. *Solar Bones* won the 2016 Goldsmiths Prize for fiction and was also named the Eason Book Club Novel of the Year at the 2016 Bord Gáis Energy Irish Book Awards. He currently lives with his wife in Galway, where he teaches on the MA in Writing at NUIG. He also teaches on the MFA in Creative Writing at the American College in Dublin.

The Writers

Martha Ashwell was born and educated in Manchester. She began writing seriously following her retirement and published her first book, *Celia's Secret: A Journey towards Reconciliation*, in 2015. She is working on an historical novel set in Northern Ireland, based on research she carried out into her Irish connections while writing *Celia's Secret*. She is also writing a series of children's books in collaboration with her daughter, Clare. She is a member of Manchester Irish Writers and the Historical Novel Society.

Bridie Breen is an Athlone-born human-rights poet who finds inspiration in ordinary life and people's stories. Planted by choice in Manchester at the age of twenty-one, she worked for thirty-four years as a psychiatric nurse in the city. She has been a member of Manchester Irish Writers for many years and is also a member of Blackwater Poetry Group. Her poetry and short stories have appeared in several anthologies, including *A Stone of the Heart* (2002), *Drawing Breath* (2004), *Changing Skies* (2014) and *The Day the Mirror Called* (2014). In 2015 she was a recipient of an inaugural Heart of Ireland Award in recognition of her contribution to Irish cultural and social life in Manchester.

Edel Burke grew up in Tuam, County Galway and now lives in Castlebar in Mayo. She lived in England in the late 1970s and early 1980s. She has been involved in a creative writing group for some years and her entry in the 2014 Over the Edge New Writer of the Year competition was highly commended by the judges.

Elizabeth Byrne is a writer and documentary filmmaker. She completed an MA in Creative Writing at the Seamus Heaney Centre, Queen's University Belfast in 2015. Before that she worked for BBC Current Affairs for ten years, producing and directing programmes for the *Panorama* and *Spotlight* strands, and films for BBC Three and BBC Four. Her 2014 film, *Panorama: Britain Under Water*, won a United Nations International Award for Best Investigative Story. Originally from Dublin, she now lives in Belfast and is slowly mastering the local art of the tray-bake.

Rebecca Crawford was awarded an MA in English with Creative Writing by Queen's University Belfast in 2016. Born in 1994, she lives in semi-rural County Down with her family. An avid writer and strong believer in the power of words, she was first published at the age of sixteen in *Take a Break's Fiction Feast*. 'From Peru to Portaferry' is based on research she carried out in British and Australian newspaper archives, which was inspired by her discovery of the gravestone of Henry Maxwell in Templecranny Cemetery in Portaferry, County Down.

Bernadette Davies-McGreal was born in Hampstead in London in 1963 to Welsh and Irish parents. She emigrated to her father's native land of Westport, County Mayo in 2007. She writes fiction, non-fiction and poetry and has been keeping diaries since the early 1980s. 'Homecoming How Ar' Ya!' is based on her father Martin, who passed away shortly after it was completed, and is dedicated to his migrant experience.

Susannah Dickey is a final-year student of English with Creative Writing at Queen's University Belfast. A native of Northern Ireland, she moved to Birmingham at eighteen to study Law for three years. Although she came to view England as an adoptive home, her poems are inspired by the initial feelings of isolation she experienced upon moving to England. 'Initiation' addresses the incongruity and internal conflict that resulted from having immersed herself in a culture alien to her origins.

Rosemary Donnelly has lived in Ballycastle, Swindon, Brighton and Belfast. She has been a teacher and a guidance counsellor who has worked with all age groups. She is a country girl who adapted to city life but never lost her roots. This, she feels, gives her an understanding of how people relate to each other and are interdependent. Rosemary is interested in capturing the essence of life experience in poetry and prose.

Des Farry is originally from Omagh, County Tyrone. Apart from spells in Birmingham and London, he has been resident in Manchester since his student days in the late 1960s. He has worked as a teacher and as a corporate finance manager. His interest in writing dates back to his teenage years, when he wrote local news notes for the *Ulster Herald* for a grand fee of one farthing per line.

Susan Graham was born near Manchester in the 1950s and now lives in Mayo. Having a foot in each country, straddling the Irish Sea, can cause discomfort but it also allows her to draw inspiration and energy from both sides. She writes for pleasure.

Kathleen Handrick is a wife, mother, grandmother and novice writer. She has always lived in Oldham, though her Irish roots are in Mayo. Her father emigrated from Lacken in the 1920s, whilst her mother was an Oldhamer whose ancestors migrated from rural Suffolk to Lancashire in the 1840s to work in the cotton mills. After retiring from a career as a primary schoolteacher, Kathleen became a volunteer at the Irish World Heritage Centre. She joined Manchester Irish Writers in 2014 and contributed to the group's anthology, *Changing Skies*, published the same year.

Clodagh Brennan Harvey holds a PhD in Folklore and Mythology from the University of California, Los Angeles, with specialisations in Irish oral narrative and Celtic Studies. She has conducted extensive field research all over Ireland with traditional storytellers, resulting in the publication of *Contemporary Irish Traditional Narrative: The English Language Tradition* (University of California Press, 1992), which is recognised as a landmark study of this area of traditional culture. She has also worked extensively for over two decades with performers of the international storytelling revival, coordinating public arts courses, festivals, workshops and lecture series, as well as performing at numerous storytelling events. Poetry is the focus of her current writing.

Alrene Hughes was born in Enniskillen, grew up in Belfast and now lives in Manchester. She co-founded Manchester Irish Writers with Rose Morris in 1994 and her fiction and poetry have been published in anthologies and broadcast on radio. She was an English teacher for twenty years and now writes full time. She is the author of a trilogy of bestselling novels, *Martha's Girls* (2013), *The Golden Sisters* (2015) and *A Song in my Heart* (2016), all published by Blackstaff Press.

Therese Kieran is from South Armagh but has settled in Belfast, where she graduated from art college in the late 1980s. She began her design career in London and moved back to Belfast in 1992. She has several family members who have emigrated to Britain and America. She has been a member of the Crescent Arts Centre writing group in Belfast since 2011.

Robert Kirk is married to Isabel and lives in Ballygowan, County Down. He began writing poetry in 2008 after completing a BA (Honours) in Literature with the Open University.

Christine Leckey lives in County Down, is retired and has two adult sons.

Ruth Mac Neely was born in Castlebar, County Mayo but grew up in London in the 1950s and 1960s. At the age of fourteen she made a decision after a holiday 'at home' that she would live in Mayo; she eventually got there when she was twenty-three. She was a special needs teacher for a number of years before going on to help set up the Mayo Rape Crisis Centre in 1994. She retired in 2014. London is now a 'second home', the place where two of her siblings have always lived and to where both of her sons have moved.

Sheila A. McHugh was born in Achill Island, County Mayo and still lives there. Her research and writing reflect the history of Achill and in particular the effect of emigration on the people and the landscape. The writer and socialist activist Peadar O'Donnell was a frequent visitor to her grandparents' home and was a mentor to her father.

Kevin McMahon lives in Manchester but his roots are in County Mayo. His poetry has been broadcast by the BBC and he won the Listowel Writers' Week New Writing Award for short stories in 1998. After retiring from his role as a college principal, he returned to the Manchester Irish Writers, with whom he writes poetry, short stories and scripts. He is also working on a novel set in Mayo.

Séamus McNally is a native of Louisburgh, County Mayo and now lives in Westport. He is a playwright and author of humorous verse, which he 'writes to recite'. He spent three summers working in Brighton in the early 1970s and ten years later spent three years in Surrey, broadening his nursing qualifications.

Bernadette Mee-Keaveney was born in Castlebar, County Mayo at the end of the Second World War and grew up there. From schooldays she was fond of English and she also has a great love of Irish, despite not being fluent in the language.

Geraldine Mitchell was born in Dublin and worked as teacher and journalist in France, Algeria and Spain before settling on the Mayo coast in 2000. She has since published two collections of poems, *World Without Maps* (Arlen House, 2011) and *Of Birds and Bones* (Arlen House, 2014).

Ann Moran is from the west of Ireland and has a background in fine art. She lives in Turlough, County Mayo with her husband and daughter.

Rose Morris was born near Dungannon in County Tyrone. Now retired from a career in art and design education in Greater Manchester schools, she devotes her time to pursuing her creative interests and community projects in Manchester and Tyrone. She co-founded Manchester Irish Writers in 1994 with Alrene Hughes and continues to co-ordinate the group's literary, dramatic and publishing activities. Her short stories, monologues and poems have been included in the group's published collections, including *At the End of the Rodden* (1997), *The Retting Dam* (2001), *A Stone of the Heart* (2002), *Drawing Breath* (2004) and *Changing Skies* (2014).

Annemarie Mullan is a professional artist and a Masters graduate of the Creative Writing programme at Queen's University Belfast. She regularly facilitates poetry workshops with Community Arts Partnership and exhibits her ceramic sculptures in Belfast and Donegal.

Denis O'Sullivan has contributed poems to a number of anthologies published by the Community Arts Partnership and Shalom House Poetry in Belfast, of which he is a founder member. He has also had several short stories published, notably in *Ireland's Own*, the BBC's *My Story* and the *Black Mountain Review.*

Ger Reidy was born near Westport in County Mayo. He has published three collections of poetry, for which he has won several national awards. His collection *Before Rain* (Arlen House, 2015) was shortlisted for the 2015 Pigott Poetry Prize at the Listowel Writers' Festival.

Kathy Ryder is a native of Tiernaur, Mulranny, County Mayo and now lives near Westport, having travelled and worked abroad for many years. She has been writing – mostly memoir and poetry – for more than twenty years, and her work has been published in *Ireland's Own* and broadcast on Midwest Radio. 'Leaving Ireland' is the emigration story of the Horan family of Newfield, Tiernaur.

Emma Savage is from Newtownards, County Down. Born in 1996, she is currently studying English with Creative Writing at Queen's University Belfast.

Annette Sills was born in Wigan, Lancashire to parents from County Mayo. Her short stories have been longlisted and shortlisted in a number of competitions, including the Fish Short Story Prize and the *Telegraph* Short Story Club. Her first novel, *The Relative Harmony of Julie O'Hagan* (2015), was awarded a publishing contract with Rethink Press after it was shortlisted in their 2014 New Novels competition. Annette lives in Manchester with her husband and two children.

Patrick Slevin has been writing poems and stories for many years. He was born in Oldham in 1973. His father comes from Westport, County Mayo.

Paul Soye is the author of the plays *Cherished* and *The Birdcage*, the latter of which won the Esso New Play Award at the Irish National Drama Festival in 1996. In 2002 he was shortlisted for the BBC's Tony Doyle Award and his play *In Irons* has been broadcast on RTÉ Radio. His novel, *The Boy in the Gap*, was published by Liberties Press in 2011.

Laura Sproule completed a degree in English and Creative Writing at Queen's University Belfast in 2016. She is very interested in the themes of culture and identity and in the future she hopes to travel throughout Britain and the US working as a writer/actor.

Gráinne Tobin has contributed to the anthologies *Word of Mouth* (Blackstaff Press, 1992) and *When the Neva Rushes Backwards* (Lagan Press, 2014). Her two poetry collections from Summer Palace Press are *Banjaxed* (2001) and *The Nervous Flyer's Companion* (2010).

Ann Marie Towey was born in Manchester. Both her parents came from Mayo and their Manchester home was always full of the extended family and visitors from 'home', with their wit, humour and stories. She is now retired, having taught English in a Manchester high school. She joined Manchester Irish Writers in 2006 and has contributed short pieces to their annual Irish Festival events, many of which are influenced by her sense of cultural dichotomy.

Mary Walsh was born in South Armagh and educated at the Sacred Heart School in Newry, County Down. A state registered nurse, she worked in hospitals in Manchester and Salford before embarking on a career as an English teacher in schools in Bolton and Middleton. She retired in 2004, since when she has been a member of Manchester Irish Writers.

LIAM HARTE

Introduction: Home and Elsewhere

To 'belong' in Ireland is to leave.
Blake Morrison, *Things My Mother Never Told Me* (2002)

People and nations have always been restless, forever scattering and gathering. Out of Africa the whole world was created. Migration and movement are synonymous and always imply a rupture of some sort. Characteristically, migration creates a breach in the individual's sense of self. To uproot from the landscape and community one is born into is to embark on an undetermined journey that challenges identity and changes one's sense of self, whether these outcomes are wished for or not. Migration is also a kind of translation from one bordered life to another. It can make the migrant lose the ability to communicate deeply, fully, with the people they leave behind, the people they love. Whether chosen or coerced, an individual's first relocation across national frontiers brings with it an exposure to difference, an entry into foreignness, a vulnerability to prejudice, a challenge to adapt. Where once there was sanctuary, continuity and the familiarity of the fixed ground, there is now contingency, relativism and the forbidding, invigorating possibility of a fresh beginning.

But I am already in danger of simplifying the complexities of home and elsewhere, as if they were impermeable binaries. A complicated complicity exists between a displaced person's native place and their adopted culture. No immigrant is a *tabula rasa* but neither are they passive carriers of diasporic sorrows. Deep traces of the grief of separation from known and accustomed ways can co-exist with a settled preference for staying put elsewhere. The feeling of 'at homeness' can be experienced in more than one location, or eschewed entirely by those whose lives have become defined by serial moves. The ache of homesickness can mutate into a relish for the new and unfamiliar. The longer the migrant stays away, the more likely it is that nostalgia will be offset by material comforts and the satisfactions of self-betterment, yet there may be times still when nothing but the physical act of return can quell the yearning to be back on home soil. Often, however, we return home to remember why we left, even though our dislocation of being persists. The more thresholds we cross, the more apparent it becomes that the dualities of home and estrangement are constitutive of the human condition.

Too often we privilege the expatriate's experiences over those of the left behind. We assume that those who stay at home must necessarily feel at home, fixed in a single location, unchanged by the journeys of others. In attending to the trials and tribulations of the uprooted, it is easy to take for granted the idea – the myth – that home is the place where we can unproblematically 'be' ourselves. Every time we sentimentalise home as the locus of serene belonging, we overlook its capacity to vex and to alienate and to damage. We forget too that a person can be in place geographically but out of place spiritually and emotionally, and that for those who experience home as a site of neglect, abuse or violence, leaving it can be the first step towards recovery and growth.

For these and myriad other reasons, the migrant's ledger of loss and gain remains open indefinitely, its tally continually carried over. For the creative migrant, however, the assets tend to outweigh the liabilities, particularly the asset (which is also a liability) of cultural and geographical displacement. Certainly, that is what writers themselves report. 'If literature is in part the business of finding new angles at which to enter reality,' claims Salman Rushdie, 'then once again our distance, our long geographical perspective, may provide us with such angles.'[1] 'Travelling away from home provides distance and perspective, and a degree of amplitude and liberation,' asserts Abdulrazak Gurnah. 'It intensifies recollection, which is the writer's hinterland.'[2] 'Real dislocation, the loss of all familiar external and internal parameters, is not glamorous, and it is not cool,' insists Eva Hoffmann, yet

> Being deframed, so to speak, from everything familiar, makes for a certain fertile detachment and gives one new ways of observing and seeing. It brings you up against certain questions that otherwise could easily remain unasked and quiescent, and brings to the fore fundamental problems that might otherwise simmer inaudibly in the background. This perhaps is the great advantage, for a writer, of exile, the compensation for the loss and the formal bonus – that it gives you a perspective, a vantage point. The distancing from the past, combined with the sense of loss and yearning, can be a wonderful stimulus to writing.[3]

Such remarks have a deep resonance in Ireland and an even deeper one in what James Joyce called 'our greater Ireland beyond the sea'.[4] The observation by Blake Morrison (son of a Kerry mother and a Lancashire father) that

---

1. Salman Rushdie, *Imaginary Homelands* (London: Granta Books, 1991), p. 15.
2. Abdulrazak Gurnah, 'Writing and Place', *Wasafiri*, vol. 19, issue 24 (2004), p. 59.
3. Eva Hoffmann, 'The New Nomads', in *Letters of Transit: Reflections on Exile, Identity, Language, and Loss*, ed. André Aciman (New York, The New Press, 1999), pp. 50-51.
4. James Joyce, *Ulysses*, ed. Declan Kiberd (London: Penguin, 1992), p. 427.

constitutes the epigraph to this Introduction encapsulates the deeply engrained importance of migration and diaspora to Irish culture, society and self-understanding across many centuries. As the historian Enda Delaney explains:

> Most European societies experienced migration. Some, like Germany, England, Sweden, Norway, Scotland, Italy, and Spain, had a very high incidence of emigration at particular points in time, such as the early twentieth century or the years after the Second World War. That said, no other Western European society has had a chronological range of movement as long as Ireland's, which stretches from the beginning of recorded human history to the present day. And, equally, no other Western European country could lay claim to the sheer geographical diversity of the settlement patterns over four centuries. Only a few places in the world have not had contact with the 'wandering' Irish, be it as navvies, soldiers, servants, merchants, colonial administrators, priests, or nuns.[5]

Thus, wherever we fix the pin on the map we find evidence of upheaval and dispersal, both before and after the nation-defining decade of the Great Famine and its mass migrations (1845-55). The history of this ever-fluctuating human exodus from Ireland takes in large- and small-scale outflows and has many landmark episodes, including the migration of Irish soldiers to the armies of continental Europe from the 1580s to the 1750s; the Flight of the Earls in 1607; the mass movement of Ulster Presbyterian congregations to the American colonies in the 1700s; the refugees who fled the famine of 1741; the departures that followed the rebellions of 1641 and 1798; the convict deportations to Australia from the 1780s to the 1850s; the assisted emigration schemes of the nineteenth century; the massive influx of Irish Catholics to the United States from the 1820s onwards; the legions of Irishmen and women who participated in the British Empire overseas; the emigration of southern Protestants and northern Catholics in the wake of Partition; the flight of the new Republic's poor and jobless to postwar Britain; the haemorrhaging of Northern Irish people during the Troubles; the recession-driven scattering of the 'Ryanair generation' of the late 1980s and early 1990s; and the vanishing Irish of recent years, dislodged by the aftershocks of an imploding economy and financial system. These are just some of the epoch-marking migrations that make it into the history books, yet they account for but a fraction of the millions of unremarked departures of men, women and children from every acre of the island, who, on a given day, left behind the familiar and set about adapting to the new.

5.　Enda Delaney, 'Diaspora', in *The Princeton History of Modern Ireland*, eds. Richard Bourke and Ian McBride (Princeton: Princeton University Press, 2016), pp. 490-91.

Joyce himself stands before us as the archetype of the restless artist in exile, advocate of the view that emigration can be a portal to greater understanding of one's self and one's homeland. Towards the end of *A Portrait of the Artist as a Young Man* (1916), Stephen Dedalus records in his diary a conversation he had with his friend Davin shortly before he himself departed Dublin, in which he cryptically remarked that truth is better grasped at a distance:

> *3 April*: Met Davin at the cigar shop opposite Findlater's church. He was in a black sweater and had a hurleystick. Asked me was it true I was going away and why. Told him the shortest way to Tara is via Holyhead.[6]

Whereas the link between voluntary expatriation and creative insight was central to Joyce's self-mythologisation, the very act of writing was analogous to exile for Seamus Heaney. As befits a poet who once identified himself as an 'inner émigré',[7] Heaney drew on the examples of Joyce and Saint Columb, the sixth-century missionary and scribe, to make the point that

> from the beginning to the end of the Irish tradition, there is this example of exiling yourself from the familiar in order to compose your soul – which is a parallel activity, I suppose, to composing poetry. . . . If things go well for you in an act of writing you are displaced to a distance and insulated within an elsewhere that gives you an exiled perspective on the usual. One could extend the meaning of 'exile' to include that defamiliarisation or strangeness which happens in the act of writing.[8]

The writers whose original works of poetry, fiction and non-fiction are collected in this anthology are on intimate terms with the displacements of which Heaney, Joyce and others speak. As writers, all know what it is like to become immersed in the 'flow' of inspiration, to move out into the unknown and the unforeseen, trusting to the capricious currents of the imagination. Most of these authors are also border-crossers in a literal, geographical sense. Many have first-hand experience of living in another country, in some cases for most of their lives. None has remained untouched by the effects of migration, even those who have never, or not yet, left home. Whether imagined or based on personal experience, their writings contain a kaleidoscope of meditations on the affective and material consequences of uprootings and regroundings for leavers, stayers and returners.

---

6. James Joyce, *A Portrait of the Artist as a Young Man*, ed. Seamus Deane (London: Penguin, 1992), p. 273.
7. Seamus Heaney, 'Exposure', in *North* (London: Faber and Faber, 1975), p. 73.
8. George Morgan, 'Interview with Seamus Heaney', *Cycnos*, vol. 15, no. 2 (2008), p. 1.

The poetry and prose collected in this anthology have their genesis in a research project funded by the UK Arts and Humanities Research Council (AHRC), which culminated in a specially commissioned play about Irish emigration being toured to cultural and community centres in the Republic of Ireland, Northern Ireland and England in May 2015. Written by Martin Lynch, *My English Tongue, My Irish Heart* is based on the autobiographical testimonies in my 2009 study, *The Literature of the Irish in Britain: Autobiography and Memoir, 1725-2001.* The two-act play traces the progress of a young, educated couple, Gary O'Donnell and Susan Hetherington, who meet at university in Galway, fall in love, fall out of love, reunite and eventually move to Manchester in the early 2000s when Gary accepts a job as a marketing executive. The birth of two children brings questions of identity and national belonging into sharp focus for the couple and confronts them with some troubling home truths. A crisis point is reached in the second act when the couple's five-year-old son shows signs of rejecting his Irish heritage. This manifests itself in his not wishing to wear the Ireland rugby jersey during an Ireland-versus-England match in the Six Nations Championship. The boy's decision to fashion his own hybrid jersey for the occasion marks his first attempt to articulate a sense of transcultural identification for which there is no ready-made emblem.[9]

The story of Gary and Susan's twentieth-first-century odyssey is intercut throughout with historical scenes based on the autobiographical sources in *The Literature of the Irish in Britain.* These scenes introduce audiences to an eclectic mix of characters – lawyers, labourers, politicians, pickpockets – whose first-person testimonies provide an oblique commentary on the lives and dilemmas of the play's contemporary protagonists. *My English Tongue, My Irish Heart* also draws on the rich Irish emigrant song tradition and features several songs that address the perplexities of Irish life in Britain, from Percy French's 1896 ballad, 'Mountains of Mourne', to Paul Brady's 1981 protest song, 'Nothing But the Same Old Story'.

Central to the whole research project was a desire to engage new and experienced creative writers in Ireland and Britain on the play's core themes of migration, belonging and identity. To achieve this, the theatre company that produced the play, Green Shoot Productions, and I organised a series of creative writing workshops, under the title 'Writing Migration', in three of the locations visited by the tour. The host venues were the Central Library in Belfast, the Linenhall Arts Centre in Castlebar and the Irish World Heritage Centre in Manchester. Each workshop series was facilitated by an accomplished writer who

---

9.　A full performance of the play, filmed at the Irish World Heritage Centre in May 2015, can be viewed at http://www.mycountryajourney.org/

enabled the participants to put narrative form on their perceptions, memories and experiences of emigration, using *The Literature of the Irish in Britain* as a creative stimulus and educative tool. Novelist Mike McCormack led the Castlebar workshop and poets Moyra Donaldson and John McAuliffe took charge of the Belfast and Manchester series respectively. The workshops took place over a six-week period, towards the end of which the participants and facilitators in each venue went to see a performance of the play.

Something About Home represents the literary harvest of these 'Writing Migration' workshops. The book's three sections comprise a selection of the outputs from each workshop series, together with a reflective essay by the respective workshop facilitator. The shifting tides of departure and return cut across these sections to reveal a number of common themes and reciprocal preoccupations, most of which revolve around the many subjective meanings of 'home'. While home in these works tends to be imagined as a territorially fixed and bounded site of belonging, the feelings it evokes are much more mutable and are seldom reducible to unalloyed love and affection. Indeed, there is much here that supports Clodagh Brennan Harvey's insight in her contribution, simply entitled 'Home', that the place we call home is 'the most difficult of imaginings, perhaps, after "love" itself'.

'Who would ever think he wants to make sail?' muses the mother in the poem by Christine Leckey from which this anthology takes its title, baffled that her son would wish to uproot himself from his secure family environment. Her question elicits an oblique response from the unsettled daughter in Laura Sproule's 'Blank Canvas': 'This place where I am – / and have always wanted to be – / it's all I dreamt of / but it's not home to me.' The palpable relief that the London-based protagonist of Elizabeth Byrne's 'Finding Home' experiences on her arrival back in Belfast – 'I feel a pulse in my chest of something unclenching: a coiled, taut thing that I didn't even realise was there' – is not at all shared by the young London-based student in Susannah Dickey's 'Initiation', whose sense of unbelonging becomes more magnified with each return visit to her grandmother in Broughshane:

> Talking to her, I wonder about the fraying and furry ropes of family that bind me to this person. I feel that my blood and sinew has more in common with the shiny steel and pulsating lights of the London Underground than with the dusty port that trickles blue through this woman's veins.

Comparable feelings of outsiderness animate Kathleen Handrick's 'Going Home', in which an elderly migrant's hesitant attempt to reconnect with his Mayo roots serves only to heighten his sense of estrangement: 'You turned away, yearning for the city. / The close, the neighbours, the banter – the peace. // "There's nothing for me here."'

Other characters' ties to home are clouded by darker emotions. For the migrant men in Ger Reidy's 'Maybe It's Because I'm a Londoner' and Séamus McNally's 'Ebb and Flow', home is synonymous with unresolved tensions and family conflicts over land and inheritance. The laconic opening of Reidy's short story reports the fateful development that sours the relationship between two brothers and triggers a bitterness that keeps churning for a lifetime: 'There were two of us for the eighty acres when I met Bridgie. She changed everything.' 'Ebb and Flow' takes us deeper into this emotional territory by depicting the eruption of deep-seated sibling resentment in an act of calculated, cold-blooded cruelty. A similar theme is broached in Bernadette Davies-McGreal's autobiographical 'Homecoming How Ar' Ya!', in which she recalls how her father's attempt to relocate from London to his Clew Bay parish ended with him 'staring at a padlocked gate leading to his beloved home'.

Davies-McGreal is one of several authors whose work addresses the complexities of growing up second-generation Irish in Britain, and in particular the difficulty of expressing a hybrid identity in a culture that regards Irishness and Britishness as mutually exclusive categories. So ingrained was Davies-McGreal's own childhood awareness of not belonging anywhere that the liminal spaces of her North London neighbourhood became charged with symbolic import:

> We lived half way up the twenty-two storey block; in fact, you could call our family the 'in-betweeners'. Mum and Dad being a combination of Welsh and Irish contributed to the fact that wherever we went we were 'blow-ins', regarded neither as English in England, nor Irish in Ireland, nor Welsh in Wales. It didn't help that our block of flats fell between Fellows Road and Adelaide Road, which meant that our address could be one or the other, just like our nationality.

In Annette Sills' short story 'Seesaw', the eponymous children's plaything comes to symbolise a young Wigan girl's desire to bring her English and Irish identities into equipoise and restore some harmony and stability to her parents' volatile relationship. The mood of a childhood marked by spiritual hyphenation and identity confusion is also deftly evoked in Ruth Mac Neely's 'Across the River with my Father' and 'Becoming Other', the latter of which foregrounds the impact of the language and vocabulary of the parental generation on a second-generation Irish child's sense of belonging:

The mystery of *Irish* took many years to solve. She knew it had to do with this place called *home*. The people around who called to see them or whom they visited on occasion were always talking about *home*. So the house where she lived with her parents was not *home*.

The heightened attunement of the second-generation ear to the relationship between language, speech and identity is also registered in Kevin McMahon's poem 'Limbo', which explores the emotions stirred up in a Manchester-Irish boy when faced with an intimate language test while 'home on holidays' in Ireland. The epiphany the poem builds towards suggests that the speaker's sense of linguistic inadequacy may be the portent of a permanently displaced self:

I knew that moment
That I was in a boundary-land
Caught between the tones
Of desire and necessity
And lost to both my worlds.

Even though his accent is 'unalloyed Cockney', the frequent flyer we encounter at Gatwick Airport in Susan Graham's 'Legacy' resembles a grown-up version of this deracinated Mancunian, especially when he confesses: '"This airport is probably the closest thing to home. More like a half-way house. I don't belong here and I don't belong there, not with my accent."'

This theme of accent perception also crops up in poems and stories that deal with the Northern Irish experience in England. Whereas the absence of an Irish brogue problematises the claims of the second generation to an Irish identity, the sound of a Northern Irish accent in England can create a different kind of dissonance, as Susannah Dickey's 'Home' attests:

I stumble and stutter and strive for acceptance.
My vowels, flat and heavy, permeate the dense air.
The natives look on with interest
at me, the invasive species.
What I say matters less than how I say it.

To the speaker in Annmarie Mullan's 'Elsewhere', the native reaction to her accent is more disapproving than curious, forcing her 'to nip and tuck' her speech, often without success. Vocal proficiency brings its own problems, however, as the Ballycastle-born narrator of Rosemary Donnelly's 'Stumbling into Swindon' explains: 'I worried that I might be adopting an English accent: this would be considered false at home.'

Languages, accents and speech patterns are carried across borders by migrants; so too are material things, from everyday items to keepsakes and treasured heirlooms to which layers of memory are attached. Significant objects dot the homely landscapes conjured up in these poems and stories: a pot of shamrocks in Rosemary Donnelly's 'Home Thoughts'; a blackthorn stick in Therese Kieran's 'Shrine'; a shawl in Bernadette Mee-Keaveney's 'Annie's Story'; an unremarkable bowl in Mary Walsh's 'The Yellow Bowl'. Each is a vivid metaphor of belonging and a powerful activator of memory – a tangible link to past homes, lost landscapes, departed people.

But perhaps the most affective recreator of home away from home for the migrant is food. 'The materiality of home-making often centres on food', observes Mary Gilmartin, who goes on to cite studies that highlight Irish migrants' 'belief in the superiority of some food from their place of origin, such as dairy products or meat, as well as an attachment to familiar and local brands, such as Tayto crisps, red lemonade and Barry's tea'.[10] Intriguingly, it is an attachment to bread that testifies to the centrality of food in several of these characters' idealisations of home, thus reminding us that the word 'company' is derived from the Latin 'com', meaning 'together', and 'panis', meaning 'bread'. 'I missed homemade Irish bread', recalls Donnelly's narrator. 'Wheaten and soda farls, pancakes and slims made on the griddle. English bread seemed to be entirely made with too much yeast, which I was not used to; it did not agree with me.' It is soda bread that satisfies Davies-McGreal's father's hunger after a Saturday afternoon tipple, and a cargo of the wheaten variety that is ferried across the water in Gráinne Tobin's 'Bread and Jam':

> Leaving for England years later to visit the grandparents
> of your hybrid children with their transplanted father,
> your car boot is searched at the docks for explosives and found instead
> to contain several loaves of wheaten bread.
> And here is what the searcher said.
> *They all pack bread. You can't get decent bread in England.*

These loaves, emblems of cultural authenticity, might be the 'Floury farls' that are gratefully devoured in Alrene Hughes' 'Soda Bread', the ending of which makes clear that, for this speaker at least, no modern-day equivalent can nourish the spirit like the memory of the original: 'There's soda bread in Tesco's now. / I never buy it.'

---

10. Mary Gilmartin, *Ireland and migration in the twenty-first century* (Manchester University Press, 2015), p. 129.

My chief hope in compiling this anthology is that, in addition to giving pleasure, these writers' searching meditations on home, belonging and identity will prompt readers to reflect more deeply on the nature, meaning and effects of migration, at a time of heightened awareness of the hazardous challenges faced by the migrant Other on a national, European and global scale. I could not have known at the outset of this project that it would result in such a productive coming together of so many writers, both emergent and established, of such manifest talent and ability, under the guidance of three excellent workshop leaders. It is they who are collectively responsible for bringing this richly varied volume to life, and I thank them sincerely for their commitment, generosity and dedication. I also thank Ruth Gonsalves Moore, Project Manager at Green Shoot Productions in Belfast, Orla Henihan, Arts Access Officer at the Linenhall Arts Centre in Castlebar and Gill Gourley, General Manager at the Irish World Heritage Centre in Manchester, for their valuable organisational input into the 'Writing Migration' workshop series. My gratitude also goes to the AHRC for the Follow-on Funding Award (AH/L014904/1) that enabled me to pursue this project, and to the University of Manchester for providing matched funding. Lastly, I want to thank publisher William Nolan, Emeritus Professor of Geography at University College Dublin, for recognising the value of this anthology by accepting it for publication, and the team at Keystrokes Digital for their technical expertise.

Each author in *Something About Home* is on an imaginative journey of discovery. Each work is the product of a journey from original conception to final publication. It is now for us, as readers, to cross the threshold between the homely and the strange and explore where these migrant trails might lead.

I

'From Belfast,
if I'm not mistaken . . .'

from 'Obduro'
Robert Kirk

MOYRA DONALDSON

Emigration: Loss and Gain

Further back than my grandparents, I know nothing about my family tree. Rather, I have created a history for myself, based on family names – Stewart, Crawford, Donaldson – and see myself as being from Scottish stock. The actual verifiable truth of it has never seemed of much importance to me. I have imagined ancestors for myself, peopled my past with men and women who moved from Scotland to Ireland, and who over the generations have made this place their home. Planters. Unwelcome immigrants.

Among the current generation of my family, close and extended, no one has emigrated or moved very far from their place of birth. It seems as if once we got here, we weren't for moving again, so the theme of emigration is not one to which I have given much thought. Of course I'm aware of the underlying issues: famine, religious freedom, economic necessity. I have read about the coffin ships, *The Eagle Wing*, the American wake, the building of the roads of England. One of the songs that my mother sang to me as a child was Percy French's 'Mountains of Mourne' – the naive emigrant thinking the streets of London would be paved with gold. It was only when I took on the role of facilitating these creative writing workshops in the spring of 2015 that I began to think in more depth about emigration and its impact on both the individual and the collective psyche.

Under the umbrella of Green Shoot Productions, the process around the workshops worked extremely well. Firstly, it was a self-selecting group of individuals, all of whom had expressed an interest in the topic. Participants came from a wide range of places and backgrounds, and there was a good age spread, from students to retirees. Gender-wise, the majority was female, but there were two men in the group. In what came as a surprise to me, most of the participants had been emigrants at some point in their lives, whether being moved to England as children by their parents, studying at English or Scottish universities, or moving for economic reasons – to find work, or better opportunities. One participant, originally from the United States, described herself as a 'professional emigrant'. When participants brought pieces of creative work to the group for feedback, the responses were always considered and helpful. Some people were new to the workshop process; all were treated with the same respect and interest. Attention was paid to the creative process, to intent, to craft and to the communication of ideas, history and emotional truths through a piece of writing.

Secondly, we had Liam Harte's book, *The Literature of the Irish in Britain:*

Autobiography and Memoir, 1725–2001, which provided a wealth of story and insight, sparking and informing a lot of our discussions. This book of autobiographical pieces revealed a rich and layered history of emigration, showing the complexity of the Irish experience in Britain through stories that spanned almost three hundred years. In turn, this encouraged us in the workshops to look beyond the simplistic and received wisdom of folktale and song, and to examine our own, actual, multi-faceted experiences – the losses and gains of emigration.

Thirdly, the group had the opportunity, mid-workshops, to attend a performance of Martin Lynch's play, *My English Tongue, My Irish Heart*. The play, which is a re-telling in a theatrical setting of some of the stories in the book, used dance, song and dialogue to bring these to life, cross-cut by one modern couple's dilemma – to stay or to go. The play had a great energy, and cleverly intertwined past and present. This provoked a lot of discussion within the group about theatrical techniques and devices, and seeing the stories treated in this way encouraged the group to consider how they would approach the subject from an artistic point of view. Some chose prose, and some poetry; some used memoir, and others used fiction. Some participants were tempted to try a genre different to the one in which they usually worked. There was an intensity of purpose in the group to respond thoughtfully and creatively.

A high level of trust and respect developed in the group, and this allowed for the sharing of heartfelt stories and memories. The discussions were wide-ranging and informed. For example, we looked at research that showed that the Irish in London have traditionally suffered from high levels of depression and mental ill health, and at the reluctance of communities to 'take back' elderly emigrants if they wanted to return home. Participants shared articles and pieces of writing that they had come across, and we teased out many themes. Cross-generational similarities were noted. Denis O'Sullivan, for example, now retired, had gone as a young man to look for work in England, and wrote evocatively of the experience of getting the boat from Belfast to Heysham in Lancashire:

> The brave men at the bar
> clutch their black pints
> tell tales as far-fetched as themselves
> sink into a sea of nostalgia
> as Ireland disappears into the dark.

('Next')

Laura Sproule, a student, and just about to start out on her working life, described looking at her local town and seeing all the closed shopfronts with pictures of shops pasted over the windows, and coming to the recognition that her best chances lay in moving away for work. Her poem, 'Blank Canvas', illustrates the losses and gains in such a move. Christine Leckey brought us the experience of being the one left behind, writing poignantly about watching her sons leave:

> I try not to dwell, but every time
> I think of you leaving something happens
> to my heart.

> ('Grieving Without a Body')

Those of the group who had experienced living in a different country spoke passionately about how it had changed them: what they had lost, but also what they had gained from the experience. We spoke a lot about the sadness that making the decision to emigrate brought with it, both for those who felt they had to leave and for those left behind. We also spoke of the sense of anticipation and excitement at the prospect of new beginnings and opportunities. We spoke of the courage it takes to up and leave. We imagined what it might have been like for the pioneer wives, packing their entire lives into a covered wagon and setting out into a hostile unknown. An inscription on an old gravestone in Templecranny Cemetery, Portaferry – 'Sacred also to the above named Henry Maxwell who departed this life at the Chincha Islands on 4th June 1855 while in command of the ship *Asia*. His remains were interred here on 1st January 1856' – led Rebecca Crawford to research this story in British and Australian newspapers and then to compose her own story, 'From Peru to Portaferry', in which she lets her imagination riff on the adventures of Captain Maxwell and his crew.

One of the aspects in which I was particularly interested was whether emigration from Ireland to England was felt differently by Northern Protestants. After all, if you see yourself culturally and politically as part of the UK, growing up with British TV, politics and cultural references, do you feel as if you are emigrating when you move from Northern Ireland to 'the mainland'? Or are you simply moving from one part of the UK to another? In discussion, it became clear that no matter how we may see ourselves, to most people in England we are all Irish, and what on the surface seems to be a very similar culture soon reveals its differences.

In 'Obduro', Robert Kirk writes movingly of his days as a schoolboy in England in the 1960s. In his piece, the boy is met with hostility in the English school: 'A boy from the back shouted, "Do you have pigs in the parlour?" Another piped up, "Do you have chickens in the kitchen and rats in the thatch?"' In 'Stumbling into Swindon', Rosemary Donnelly recalls: 'I expected England to be just like home but found that almost everyone I met found my North Antrim accent difficult to understand and incomprehensible on the telephone.' Writers in the group also spoke of the dark days of the Troubles when there was no nuance possible: you were simply a Paddy and a potential threat, whether you saw yourself as nationalist, unionist or nothing at all.

One of the concepts that we spent a long time considering was that of 'home'. Elizabeth Byrne brought us the idea of *seisin*, an Old English word that includes in its meaning the idea of a land and people laying claim to the individual. In 'Finding Home', she writes: 'It was a shared moment, an acknowledgement of belonging, of being somehow let in. It was not simply something you were given or took. It was something that happened to you, something you chose to accept, and afterwards, you had a place that was yours.' We discussed this concept and through it understood that even as an emigrant, it is possible to feel 'at home' in a foreign country, given time.

From a personal point of view, I found this a very interesting idea, as although I have always lived in Northern Ireland, I have spent a large part of my life not feeling at home here. One of the first poems I wrote, 'Exile', reflected this feeling. These workshops left me wondering why it had never really occurred to me to move away. I may have thought about it on occasions but never with any real intent. What was it that rooted me here through all the decades of conflict and feelings of internal exile, of not belonging? I have no definitive answer, but I do have a clearer realisation that something in me could not imagine anywhere else feeling like home either. It is a recognition of my ongoing need to come to some sort of accommodation with the troubled place of my birth.

Exile

What ground is mine
if I would govern myself?
Where, is my country
if neither bogs nor gantries
speak of me?
Where can I stand
if I am not one thing or the other?

My grandfather knew where he stood.
Ancestors planted his feet
in fertile soil, green futures were
named in his name, possessed.
He preached their flinty faith in
Mission Tents, visions of eternal life

on soft Ulster evenings,
but there was no redemption.
Not in the land or through the Blood.
Not in the harsh lessons of duty, obedience
with which he marked his children.

He is stripped of virtue,
his legacy a stone
of no magic, no transcendence.
No children ever turn to swans,
wafer remains wafer on the tongue,
and flesh is always flesh.

My two white birds will bring me
water from the mountains,
beakfuls of sweet sips.
I will grow a new tongue,
paint my body with circles
and symbols of strength, mark myself
as one who belongs in the desert.

(from *Snakeskin Stilettos*, 1997)

Over recent years, and largely as a result of the peace process and the movement towards a more liberal society, this desert feeling has changed for me, and I feel as if I have had that moment of *seisin*, that acknowledgement of belonging, of the land of my birth finally claiming me as its own.

Movilla Cemetery

It's beautiful here, high as Scrabo's crag and tail,
looking down on the lough of many harbours
and across to the Mournes, landscape singing
through the bones; chromatic scale of home.

Easter, Christmas, anniversaries, the living come,
each to their own: *beloved husband; dearest daughter;*
each *sadly missed.* They bring flowers and dampened
cloths to wipe the gravestones clear of droppings, moss.

Remembering and forgetting, memory and dust.
Century upon century of story: Ulster kings; Finian
and the word of Christ; the war hero; the provost;
my mother, who thought it was a cold place, always

wanted to be returned to an earlier belonging.
She's contented here at last, accepting of the earth
and my father lying beside her, for it's my story
now; for a time I am the word and the telling of home.

I will be buried here, in the grave my husband bought.
Belonging sings to me here, and I am singing back.

(from *The Goose Tree*, 2014)

Of course I realise I was fortunate to be able to make the choice to stay; for some, the choice is made for them through circumstances well beyond their control. There was a consensus in the group that the process encouraged everyone not only to examine Irish emigration but also to think more deeply about current emigration issues worldwide, about the terrible circumstances that global politics, war and poverty have imposed on so many people.

It was a real pleasure to facilitate these workshops and they produced many fine pieces of work, as evidenced by this book. They also spoke to the fact that the process can be as important as the end product. Great discussions and thoughtful input from all the participants led to insights, a shared sense of understanding and a thoroughly enjoyable experience.

CHRISTINE LECKEY

Something About Home

Identical to every other house along this street
and two or three streets over, he knows which one is his.
He feels its tug, is carried towards it by the tide,
from far further than the end of his road.

Moored to Mother and Father,
berthed with a brother,
an ordinary family in an ordinary house
set on a reliable course.
Who would ever think he wants to make sail?

Goodbye by Degrees

It started young. He was five years old,
a bomb attack on the village police,
his school, his house, collateral damage.
Bombs in the market town
near to where his Mum would be
The nights she worked he stayed awake
'When I'm old enough, I'm out of here.'

Unwilling to carry the weight
of hatred and history, he bided his time.
When it came, it was university,
what his family wanted. No contest
Off to London for study, and more study,
to become what he hopes he wants to be
A Londoner will do, they come
in so many different colours and kinds.
What is one more Irishman?

Grieving Without a Body

I decided what you liked to eat, what you wanted
to wear, books to read, games to play.
It was me you came to, to fix what was broken:
toys, bones, all the way to heart and ego.

My clearest view of you, my son, is over my shoulder,
back to a picture imperfectly drawn from memory,
a wondrous construction, my soft place of retreat
where I allow myself to think I really knew you.

I try not to dwell, but every time
I think of you leaving something happens
to my heart. It falls, then rises, swells, fit to burst
beyond its capacity to hold you within it.

*

This is not missing my baby, my boy all grown up.
Going to another country is another kind of missing.
Time was I couldn't bear the thought of you off to school.
Now it will take a plane or a boat if I need to reach you.

Distance tears holes that yawn into a void
and I am left to mourn the empty space.

Denis O'Sullivan

Neutral

I think it was the bomb that flew over
the barracks wall in Union Square, Cork
that made my grandfather's mind up.
It may have been the indignity of
the outside privy door being blown off
while he was reading the *Irish Times*
that saw him and his young wife bound
for Dún Laoghaire and the ferry to Holyhead
with his Royal Irish Constabulary uniform
swapped for Royal Engineers' gear,
my father cosseted in my granny's womb.
Years later, when they returned to Belfast
to ensure their child was brought up Irish,
a fire bomb, compliments of Adolf Hitler,
fell down their modest chimney.
The family survived but my grandmother
was forever mortified at the effrontery
of her, a neutral, being mistaken for a Brit.

Evelyn

She was always different from my other aunts,
startlingly blue eyes, flaxen hair,
a ready smile to grace her welcoming.

She could have passed for country folk
with her gracious offering of new griddled
wheaten slathered in melting butter,
washed down with fresh-brewed tea or
buttermilk from the muslin-covered churn.

Uncle John, a gentle soul with a heart of corn,
brought her home to Leggygowan
when he left the factories of Liverpool behind
and settled to selling shoes in Saintfield.

At her funeral, I first heard of the father
who had passed on his Scandinavian genes,
the smoke-blue eyes, the platinum hair.

Next

From the shed's high ceiling
fluorescent light glimmers
through dank evening mist
roiling off the Lagan's waters
like ghostly serpents.

The line moves at snail's pace
on the officious direction
of uniformed ticket collectors
under the suspicious gaze
of ever-watchful policemen.

Like patient cattle on the farms
they come from, they wait
to be called forward, their tickets
examined, anxious moments
before being nodded through.

The narrow gap in the shed doors
the opening onto the dock
entry to a future unknown
where the same tongue
sounds foreign in a strange land.

The harbour lights fade to nothing
as the thrum of the ship's engines
rises to meet the incoming swell
and the shore slips stealthily
away in the gleaming wash.

In the cabin bodies are everywhere
seeking comfort on wooden benches
or propped like ragged bundles
against bulkheads, thoughts far off
in turf-warmed kitchens.

The brave men at the bar
clutch their black pints
tell tales as far-fetched as themselves
sink into a sea of nostalgia
as Ireland disappears into the dark.

In the bitter air of a Heysham morning
the train waits steam-enshrouded
for the human cargo to scrabble aboard
desperate to avoid the misery
of standing all the way to Crewe.

We whistle through a clutter
of towns and villages, stunned
by the expanse of greenery
in between, certain it is not
as green as the land we left behind.

Names that don't roll off the tongue,
Lichfield, Nuneaton, Rugby, Northampton,
Shrewsbury, Birmingham, Milton Keynes.
A foretaste of problems to come
in a nation of small shopkeepers.

The seemingly never-ending succession
of houses, backs turned scornfully
to the tracks, gardens variously tidy
and untidy, a soot-filled pall of steam
threatening occasional clotheslines.

A jigsaw of lines and junctions
plays tricks on tired eyes and brains
twisting and turning, racketing
through points and signals to the
cold grey platforms of Euston.

ROBERT KIRK

Obduro

First day at Heieson Secondary School in Ramsgate did not go well, for when walking through school gates decorated with a poster advertising a showing of last summer's World Cup victory by England over West Germany, I found myself surrounded by several bigger boys. It was obvious they'd been awaiting my arrival: my English cousin, Stephen, had tipped them off. I could see him at the back of the crowd, a smug grin on his fat face. I'd lived at Aunt Joyce's house for several weeks until suitable foster care was found: there was a lot of enmity when Stephen and I parted.

'He's not that big. The way you told it, Stevey, I thought he'd be a giant,' one of the boys said, 'so I can't believe this little shit of a Paddy bested you.'

Stephen had stopped grinning.

'My name isn't Paddy! It's Richard!'

'It is to me. This is my patch. What I say goes. So get used to it, turf-digger, or else!'

The other boys laughed. A boy from the back shouted, 'Do you have pigs in the parlour?' Another piped up, 'Do you have chickens in the kitchen and rats in the thatch?' And in a poor attempt of a Dublin accent, 'Begorrah Mary and Martha, I'm starvin', get me some spuds and buttermilk.'

The taunts attracted others. They stood and watched as What-I-say-goes and his cronies closed in like hounds cornering a fox. They started pushing me. I stepped backwards and felt iron railings press against my back. I hunkered down, expecting a kicking. Instead, someone grabbed my tie; I felt it tighten until I could hardly breathe. Another tore the badge from my blazer. Then I heard their yells of glee as they tossed my school bag into the air, its contents scattering the ground; then trod on new jotters and books covered in brown paper. I watched Stephen pick up pencils and pens and throw them over the railings. Then came the chanting, 'Paddy the turf digger! Paddy the turf-digger!' Someone shouted, 'Scram, old Eco's coming!'

'Boys, that's enough!' commanded Mr Eacott. 'Taylor, Morrison, Lutz, I'll see you in my office after assembly.'

Mr Eacott was a tall man. He wore a navy jacket two sizes too big and black baggy trousers that flapped about his legs; silver hair was swept back from his forehead; brown eyes were pools of muddy water; a large hooked nose and thin bluish lips, and a scrawny neck poked out from an oversized collar fastened with a bright blue dickie-bow.

'Are you all right, boy?' he asked.

'Yes, sir.' I was getting used to holding back the tears.

He bent down and asked, 'What's your name?'

'Richard. Richard Crooks, sir. I'm . . . I'm from Northern Ireland.'

'From Belfast, if I'm not mistaken.' Mr Eacott let slip a soft smile. 'I know that accent well. Come,' he said, 'let's get your belongings together. I'll get Miss Simmons to sew the badge back on to your blazer.' He ran a bony finger over the embroidered inscription below a white seahorse. It read 'Obduro'.

'Do you know what this means?' he asked.

'No, sir. I think it's Latin. Never did Latin at school back home.'

'It means "to persist or endure."' He took my hand, pulled me to my feet and said, 'Let's see if we can endure it together.'

Ramsgate Beach (June 1967)

In this place of soft accents,
sunlight flickers like fireflies
on the English Channel; and beyond, yellow
tongues of Goodwin Sands, forever shifting
on tide and current to swallow unwary ships,
and given time, spit them out bit by bit.

Along this shore are brown ribbons
of dried seaweed – their roots torn
from rocks which held them fast –

I lift my eyes to the hills
and they are not there.

Terminus (June 1969)

Euston Station and heat from diesel electric engines
saturates the air and mingles with my sweat-damp shirt;
an oily residue slicks my hair with a metallic stink.
In the shimmer, polished platforms are quicksilver,
where sinuous leviathans swallow and spew waves
of ghostly travellers in tune with discordant tones:
doors slamming, couplings clanking, brakes squealing,
wheels sparking and shrieking.
                    Slow time has passed
too fast. I hear a hum from the track – the boat train
from Heysham rolls into the station,
the train that will carry me back.

Rosemary Donnelly

Stumbling into Swindon

The night fog was so dense on the motorway between Belfast and Dublin that all white lines had disappeared. Then two red pinpoints of light appeared and I gratefully tucked in behind the lorry all the way to Dublin.

Never having driven further than the fifty-nine miles from my home town of Ballycastle to Belfast, driving to England to take up my first permanent job was an adventure. A recession in the late 1970s meant temporary jobs in teaching were interspersed with unemployment, which left me feeling at times useless as well as almost broke. Then a postgraduate course to become a careers guidance counsellor came up. Careers officers were recruited from within the Northern Ireland Civil Service so vacancies were not open to external applicants like myself. So instead I applied for a job in the Wiltshire Careers Service, was interviewed at head office in Trowbridge and accepted a permanent job in Swindon. I knew the Careers Service was innovative and had an excellent national reputation under the inspirational leadership of Terry Collins, who also guest-lectured on our course. Terry is a man I still fondly remember as being passionate about treating each client as if he or she were the only person you were to see that day.

However, that was in the future. I still had to navigate my way to Swindon. My third-year school atlas was to be my guide but unfortunately there were no roads on the map of England and Wales, only towns, rivers and mountains. After travelling on the ferry from Dublin to Holyhead I drove all day until I saw a sign for Portsmouth and realised I had gone too far.

The dark streets of Swindon appeared at about 11.30 PM. Near the railway station I saw a light at a bed and breakfast and asked for a room. My entire belongings were in the boot of my orange Mazda 818, a car which was not-so-slowly rusting along the driver's side. It was on its third engine, but that's another story. The landlady showed me to my room and I spent the warm September night overtired and wrestling with the nylon sheets. In the morning breakfast was served at the table in the company of friendly Irish navvies, all of us grateful for work.

I expected England to be just like home but found that almost everyone I met found my North Antrim accent difficult to understand – and incomprehensible on the telephone. I quickly learned to speak more slowly and tried to sound out my words clearly. However, I worried that I might be adopting an English accent: this would be considered false at home. After a couple of nights under the nylon sheets, I moved to another bed and breakfast nearer work and started to look for a place in a shared house. In my new abode I was the only guest. The landlady served me breakfast and an evening meal at a table where the tablecloth was folded in half so that it only covered the part of the table I sat at. For a special treat she served me faggots, a local dish made from offal. I tried to eat them but failed. Any meat I was served, or cooked myself, in Swindon seemed to have no taste – not like the rich, savoury taste of meat at home. I wondered what kind of life English cows had.

I missed homemade Irish bread. Wheaten and soda farls, pancakes and slims made on the griddle. English bread seemed to be entirely made with too much yeast, which I was not used to; it did not agree with me.

I searched the local paper each night for shared accommodation and was amazed to find that the room was always taken by the time I arrived at the house. In Belfast we would have interviewed all applicants and chosen the one who would best fit into the household.

At last I was accepted to share with two young women in a detached house in a tiny hamlet called Kingston Winslow near Shrivenham, five or six miles from Swindon. The English girls said that the house was owned by an Irishman. I went to see it at night and moved in the same night. The next morning, driving to work, I encountered a complicated roundabout known locally as 'the Magic Roundabout' because it had so many mini-roundabouts to negotiate. I had driven straight across it the previous night, and never was able to use it without being hooted at by other cars. It made no sense to me.

Returning at night from work, I would turn off the main road at Shrivenham and drive past fields on a flat narrow road. Some moonlit nights I would switch off the lights and drive on a ribbon of moonlight. Somehow, this reminded me of the natural beauty of home and I would feel joyful and just a little bit thrilled by the danger. In the mornings I passed a picture-postcard village with Tudor cottages and swans on the lake. Rounding a bend, one or two grouse would often walk slowly across the road in front of the car, for this was Oxfordshire, and hunting country.

Slowly, I made friends with four of my colleagues but somehow I still felt a stranger in a strange land. This was brought home to me one night after leaving a parents' evening in a local school. I wanted to talk to a friend so I could wind down after the long day. By this time I was living in a flat on my own. I called to an English friend unannounced and knew by the expression on her face at the door that I was not welcome. I made an excuse and then went to the door of an Irish girl I had recently met. She welcomed me in, and that is when I knew the meaning of cultural difference.

I learned not to assume that just because we had a common language and were part of the UK, life and behaviour were the same. I learned much that was useful by listening and observing. I learned to understand rather than to expect.

Home Thoughts

A pot of shamrocks
outside my back door
welcomes me home.

A gift from a friend
last year.
'Keep them in the pot,
or they will take over.'

A memory of life in England.
My mother posting me
a little pot of shamrocks
for St Patrick's Day.
Every year.

Soil and green leaf
pull me gently back
to home ground.

ELIZABETH BYRNE

Finding Home

I'm working over in London again. The plan is to move here soon; it's the logical next step for my career. It's expected, really. The last few years in Belfast were a transition, a strategic move from Dublin to get the job, a foot in the door of the BBC and the UK. But everyone knows that London is the real centre of the universe. I spend weeks at a time here anyway, and I know my way around the main places. I'm still not sure what's south and what's north, and which is better or safer. But it's all so exciting! So diverse! Cosmopolitan! Challenging! At least, that's what I say if anyone asks. I omit 'expensive', 'dirty' and 'lonely'. I don't mention that I never stay at weekends. I want to look like I am well able for it, up to the pace of it. It is hard, a lot of the time. I don't just mean difficult. I mean hard as in steel and stone and concrete and glass. The people are hard too.

But to not *like* London? To not want to be here, to find it too much, relentless, exhausting? What a failure of nerve and ambition that would be. So what if every morning I have to stand still in front of the door and force myself to take slow breaths, ignoring the fluttering in my chest, and remind myself that there is nothing to it? Millions of people do this every day, this London. Loads of them are Irish. I've lived in a city all my life. Isn't Dublin just a smaller version of this? There's a flight to catch, for God's sake. So pull it together. Stop failing. Get out there, now. Now.

Down to the lobby of the hotel, skip the congealing full English in the tray-clatter of the restaurant, pass by the vending machines of sandwiches and bitter coffee, last night's dinner. Walk out the door into the slap of the summer heat and the sticky, clogged air, already recycled through ten million other lungs. Weave around all the slow walkers on the path, wait for a gap in the traffic to get across the road, dive into the tube station and join the press of people through the turnstiles, looking down along the descending lines of backs of heads. Stand on the right. Ads at every angle alongside every step, every blink: a play you won't see, a tour you can't afford, a medicine, insurance, plastic surgery, the play again, expensive shoes, beware pickpockets, have you seen this play? The same ads as yesterday and the day before that, along every escalator in every station.

Wait on the platform, move down if it's crowded, train in two minutes, just wait. Wait. Look at the ads on the wall opposite, same as yesterday, there's nowhere else to look. The train arrives, very full, push to get on. Six stops to go. Wait. Try to hold on to the pole and not bash into the guys next to you. Five stops to go. Try to avoid looking at all the ads, all the same ones, but don't stare at anyone and don't smile. Look at coats, shoes, sides of faces, backs of heads, the front page of the *Metro* in front of a man's face, bendy reflections in the glass, your own hand. Four stops to go. More people get on.

Listen to the modulated voice of *Mind the Gap* correctly say the station names. *Thaydan Boyce. Marlibone. Hoebun. The Mal.* Remember them. Traps for an ignorant Paddy. Avoided.

Get out at Victoria Station, push along the platform, follow the crowds up the stairs along the tunnel, listen to the echoing footsteps ahead of you and the muted roar of more trains arriving below. Lift number three is next. Wait. More ads on all the walls, on every surface. The doors shut. The lift ascends. Wait.

Through the turnstile, up the steps, run across the vast concourse, stop and frantically scan the vast board to find the right platform. The next train is to Reading, Dorking, Brighton, Brixton, Croydon East, Croydon North, Folkestone, Herne Hill, Southampton, Gatwick Airport. Run. Ignore the smells of Cornish pasties, burgers, burritos, KFC, bad coffee, sweet doughnuts and thousands of people. Get on the train, collapse into a seat. Wait.

I think, as I sit here and the train starts to move, that I am doing very well. I am a functioning commuter. I lean my head against the window. I close my eyes.

Three hours later, I land in Belfast. I am one of the first people off the plane, carefully making my way down the wee wheelie steps onto the ground. Everyone thanks the crew on the way out. It's a warm evening, and the sun is just starting to get low. I walk slowly across the tarmac, through Arrivals, with its four small carousels, and down the passageway to the exit. It's cooler outside, until I pass under the shaded canopy back into the sun. The breeze catches at my hair and buffets my coat out behind me. The cloth snaps in the air like a clean sheet. I cross the car park and take a deep breath of pure, fresh air. I can smell growing things, country cattle smells, gorse and mountains. There's a cab waiting. We drive from the airport over green hills and I watch the sun dipping behind them, molten red, catching the few clouds above in watercolour gold.

Driving through Belfast, City Hall is lit up now in disco blue, illuminating the heart of the city. We pass by the front of the building and I look at the light washing over the grand stone façade, the darkened windows, the symmetry of the pillars and the pediment, and up onto the great dome. I think: tomorrow I'll come down here and just sit on the grass in the sun. I feel a pulse in my chest of something unclenching: a coiled, taut thing that I didn't even realise was there. I'm so glad to be home, I think. God I'm glad to be home.

Years ago I came across the word *seisin* in a story, an Old English word. In feudal times it meant taking possession of a fiefdom bestowed by the king, and shares roots with the word 'seize'. It's just an archaic legal term now. But in the story I read it had another, older, softer meaning. It was not only the moment that a young lord or chief came into ownership of their lands and all the people tied to them, but also the moment when those lands and people laid claim to him. It was a shared moment, an acknowledgement of belonging, of being somehow let in. It was not simply something you were given or took. It was something that happened to you, something you chose to accept, and afterwards, you had a place that was yours.

THERESE KIERAN

A Letter to Belfast

April 2015

Dear Belfast,

You are my adopted home, though I cannot claim to feel I truly belong here. I arrived when the Troubles were in full flow, but coming from where I did, this didn't faze me. I came to study, to learn the principles and practices of design. After four years' learning, there was nothing for it but to leave you; in 1989 you had little to offer by way of creative opportunity.

I quickly realised there was value in leaving to search for additional skills and experience, and to return a better proposition for any potential employer. So that's what I did, Belfast: we had a four-year courtship, then I left you. But I came back two years later ready for a long-term commitment. I'd left you for a brief fling with London, where I learned more about design than any Masters degree could have taught me. Thankfully, employment emerged from both the private and public sectors.

Belfast, you take a lot of flak. You've been accused more than once of being a backwater, the poor relation, on the hind tit, insular, not world-class. And yes, there have been a few dodgy products let loose, but there are also those that demonstrate how 'Made in Belfast' can compete on a world stage.

Belfast, you are a strange mixture of the best of the best and the worst of the worst. You are rooted in the past but committed to a future that aims to bring about positive change and development. You have a charm that endears me to you; a vulnerability that scares me; a fighting spirit that is more about survival than success. Your dysfunctionality bears the scars of the past pitted against the dreams of a normal, progressive outlook. But you must be commended for your endeavours over the last fifteen years, the fruits of which have, at times, been sublime.

Undoubtedly, today your new confidence is emerging as you begin to entertain such notions as prosperity, inclusivity and blowing your own trumpet. You are beginning to trust the blow-ins like me; the curiosity of visitors who come for the Guinness, the *seisiún* and the craic, knowing very little about the Troubles but glad they are over. And how about those trusting souls, far from their native homes, who have settled, integrated and contributed to this new dawn for you? People like the Russian waitress who served me at a trendy pan-Asian restaurant last weekend, or the Polish guy who tackles the weeds in my garden, a qualified PE teacher, but happy to find work doing almost anything. I could be wrong, but

I seem to sense a greater influx of our southern neighbours too, who years ago could only be tempted across the border by a favourable exchange rate on their euros.

Though I am often frustrated with you, Belfast, with your impossibly slow pilgrimage to a new era, this one-step-forward-two-steps-back approach, I am also immensely proud. You have managed to sustain the quality of your educational and cultural centres, including Queen's University, the Lyric Theatre, the Mac, the Sonic Arts Research Centre – all of them world-class.

Your aspiring creatives sprout from the solid trunks of masters past and present: John Hewitt, John Luke, Van Morrison, David Holmes, Marie Jones, Rita Duffy, Oliver Jeffers. This small scrap of the island yields a rich and varied archive to research and inspire.

Enough, possibly, Belfast, to make me want to stay. You'll always be small, you'll always have your detractors, but forget fifty shades of fucked-up, forty shades of green, the sash your father wore and all that jazz – you've definitely got potential!

I'll end by saying that being of a certain age, I can appreciate the changes in you, Belfast, but this might not be so apparent to the young. So the opportunity is now, you produce good stock but you also haemorrhage a lot of talent – and that's OK. Send them off, let them seek new skills and opportunities elsewhere, but I'd like to think they might consider coming back one day to a place worth coming back to.

Yours . . . x

Shrine

Greeted by the rusty horseshoe smile
relic of a day so long ago,
like the blackthorn stick that guards the door
years since it slipped the cradle of my grandfather's hand;
he never made it over,
but now is here, in her Irish home:
here his soft-felted sky-piece,
here his photograph, another and another,
here painted with his pipe
surrounded by decades captured and framed,
siblings, in-laws, nieces and nephews,
the Irish lives she dipped her toes in
revived her like the waters of Lough Patrick.
In the porch the woven reeds of Brigid's cross,
in the hall the font adorned with beads,
from shelves and ledges generations fix their stare,
frozen brides and first communicants,
she made it home on their big days,
bought souvenirs on each and every visit;
here the crystal counties, Waterford, Cavan, Tyrone,
here the forked edges of new ivory Belleek,
here the mohair of Avoca, the mugs of Nicholas Mosse,
the silverware of Newbridge, the Claddagh and the cross.
And evenings when she waltzes with the brush,
jives and twists to Dickie Rock,
resurrects the 'Hucklebuck', sings ballads with Big Tom;
here the journey of her heart,
here the faces she now mourns,
here, in England, she makes her Irish home.

Susannah Dickey

Home

8. I watch my grandmother deliver a calf.
With a tug it is ripped from its lowing host,
awash with a silvery bovine viscera.
Blinking eyes echo with hollow misapprehension.
I watch it stumble on spindle legs,
braying with a breathy longing.
I am beckoned to spectate.

18. I stand in a West Midlands kitchen.
I see myself: a parochial palimpsest.
Reborn and rewritten.
I stumble and stutter and strive for acceptance.
My vowels, flat and heavy, permeate the dense air.
The natives look on with interest
at me, the invasive species.
What I say matters less than how I say it.
I yearn for home.

A Phone Call from Home

'Everything's grand.'
The words you use when your mother calls.
It becomes a recurring joke: a mantra, a motif, a moniker.
Something you say, whilst saying nothing.
She doesn't probe, she doesn't pry.
You don't divulge, you don't comply with her request.
Not because you don't love her.
Not because love isn't there, but because it threatens to devour you.

'Grand.'
The response you give when your mother asks how things are.
You talk on the phone, not across a computer screen.
So she can't see.
She can't see your unwashed hair, your purple lids, your pallid skin.
Your bulbous nose, your neck, strangled and thin with strained and violet
veins.

She can't see you shake with the pain of an untreated, infected nail.
She can't see that your room is in chaos because your life here has no order.
'Everything's grand.'
She doesn't pry, but you wonder if she knows.

'Grand.'
The word you both cling to,
because to admit the truth is to admit your failings:
You failed in convincing her you could navigate the wilderness.
She failed in letting you careen blindly into the dark.
You can't let her see that you are flailing.
She can't let you see her fractured heart.

'Everything's grand.'
Perhaps neither of you believe it.
But you pretend,
to keep the monsters at bay.

'Everything's grand.'
Just a thing I say.

Initiation

Upon arriving home there is always the customary visit to a small house in Broughshane. This acts as an initiation back into the life left behind. At university there are similar rituals, but they involve excess and hedonism: a sticky bottle of rosé and a sweat-soaked blindfold. Here they involve a conveyor belt of biscuits, a backlog of *Hello!* magazines and a different form of degradation. In a room combusting with soft furnishings and elegantly dressed figurines sits my mother's mother. Granny. *My* granny.

Talking to her, I wonder about the fraying and furry ropes of family that bind me to this person. I feel that my blood and sinew has more in common with the shiny steel and pulsating lights of the London Underground than with the dusty port that trickles blue through this woman's veins. I am often warned, prior to such reunions: 'Don't upset your granny.' These words are said in the gravest of tones: 'Don't upset your granny.' I wonder if she is mine, for the tethers seem to exist only by virtue of some intangible law. I spend these visits rehearsing a chromatic symphony of monosyllabic hums, for it seems that every word uttered is at risk of committing this cardinal sin. She speaks with a buttery, honeyed warmth, reminding me of the sticky sandwiches she used to make, but in a language that might as well be Latin, for it jars in my mind. She tars the oppressed with an invisible brush. She cuts down minorities with an invisible sword. I bristle in silence, my liberal politics held before me like an invisible aegis.

She muses aloud about my hair, my clothes, my relationship status. I respond with a laugh that trills in a minor key.

Years later, when she is taken from the small house to a larger house, to a room to be shared with other women and men, I feel our dynamic shift. I am still escorted to my initiation, but now the austere warning is gone, is spoken by my mother with a good-natured snort. Any offence imparted will be quickly forgotten.

Now, we watch television together and she purports to know every actor, presenter, host. She recounts stories that never happened, recalls people that never were, but struggles to locate my name in the dim fog of her memory. When she coughs, I am tasked with lifting a glass of water to her chin, positioning a straw between her deflated lips. Sometimes, I am over-zealous and she splutters, and I wonder at how a familial rhythm can be so set off course by just two generations.

When I sit in pubs, restaurants, cafés, engaged in the exchange of fiery words with friends, I think of Granny. I wonder: if she could witness me, what would she say? I wonder: if she had possession of her mind, what would she think? Perhaps she, like me, feels the ties between us tenuous and would simply sniff at my strange sensibilities. Perhaps she too would wonder at the structural integrity of the hereditary chain. Perhaps she sees me as a strident Persephone, half of her world, half of a dark unknown. Perhaps she would pray for the severing of the links, leaving me, a cuckoo in the familial nest, to flail, to flounder, to float away.

ANNEMARIE MULLAN

Elsewhere

The first few pangs descend
upon me, in the dark. Alone
I'd fiddle with the forecast

shiver at its late-night tally
of the wind-speed; mention
of Malin and Rockall

calling to mind the poet
who'd listened and listed all
in a softer, slower tongue

and although each day
I'd practise other voices
in the Underground –

to nip and tuck my speech –
I'd sometimes make
an awkward slip

in high-street shops
and ask for something
'wee' instead of small

then sense the glance
feel the disapproval
as I'd browse the rows

of grocery goods
with an absent air
for I already know

that all those foods –
the usual ones
I crave – aren't there.

Meanwhile, outside
a trace of smoke
upon the breeze

reminds me of autumn
in a wee town
in a country, elsewhere.

Taking the Boat

When she was grown up, she'd often thought,
she'd take the boat like all those country girls
in Edna's books who wore smart frocks
and drank fine wine with handsome men
who'd buy them flowers and dazzle them
with foreign food while they'd converse.

The first she heard when she emerged
from the distance of a general anaesthetic
were the accents of the Pakistani doctor
and the English orderly holding a radio
out the window to get the best reception
for some international cricket match.

The Irish girls in the other metal beds,
all cowed and shy, were murmuring
in soft low sleepy tones. Some moaned.
One, bolder than the rest, declared
that she had just popped out from work,
had told her boss that she was with a client.

She gave the other ones, who asked, precise
directions to a friendly hostel and the dole.
Not one was going back. They said that they
would never want to face the rest at home,
who'd know or guess why they had upped
and gone away to England in the first place.

Missed

Her noisy absence lingers
in the tiny things –

a lipstick stain upon
the cushion of a rattan chair

the hair-dyed towel we use
to wipe the bathroom floor

the odd mascara cotton bud
fished from the laundry pile.

Her crimplene dresses, pencil cases
toys and bits and bobs

are in a box. It's just a matter of time
before these go to War On Want.

She's the relatives' favourite topic
when she's missed from family snaps

and although her quarterly appointments
and voting slips still come

the strains of all-night radio have stopped
since her younger brother got her room.

Our telephone is tingling from last night's call –
says when she's more settled

she'll send a big long newsy letter
and cuttings from all her potted succulents.

LAURA SPROULE

ID

Who am I?
I am in the walls of this building
but they are not me.
I am in the teeth-marked table
the scored window
the door dented by a bike
(that should not have been brought inside)
and although they each taught a lesson
they are not me.

I am in the grass of this land too
the eldest sibling
fearlessly leading my charge
the giggling friend
poring over magazines in the summer heat
the nervous date
trying not to complain
about the wet grass under the picnic blanket.
I am from this grass
but I am not it.

I am the dream of another land
Rags to riches and a good man's hand
I am the hope of a life not yet lived
of another shore, undigging secrets well hid
I am a shaker, a mover
I love what I have lost and will love what is to come
mingled with fear and trepidation surely
but love still.
Childhood behind, adulthood in front
Ireland has given me what I have
and when I work out what I have
I'll be fine.

What I will do and where I will go?
Who will I be?
Who knows?

I Must Go

The time they wouldn't let me play,
the time they said my skin was strange,
the time I wasn't tall enough,
the time I wasn't thin enough,
the time they laughed
at what I wanted,
the words they used,
the threats they taunted.
The scars remain when the tears have gone,
they still serve to spur me on
to another land
my dreams to chase
myself to prove
my fear to lose.

Blank Canvas

This place where I am –
and have always wanted to be –
it's all I dreamt of
but it's not home to me.

Life is a blank canvas
but I miss the colours,
I miss Matt and Sue
and Tom and the others.

I miss the pink lips of that awful first kiss,
the green bruise of the rugby pass missed,
the black fuzzy love of a bouncing Rottweiler
and the spilling blue tears
over the boy who 'didn't like me' either.

Here I know where nothing is,
and though I want to find out,
sometimes I miss using words
I don't have to think about.

So in this new place
I will find my way
but oh dear Ireland
I'll be back someday.

CLODAGH BRENNAN HARVEY

Home

Fraught, freighted, full of 'f' words; the most difficult of imaginings, perhaps, after 'love' itself. I don't know if for most people 'home' is replete with soft, welcoming images – I think I have become a victim to that belief – but it is a difficult word for me. If 'home' is some place or destination where you don't have to explain yourself – and I would like it to be that – then I have not yet arrived there, but I am closer. I think my difficulty with 'home' is a result of parents who were constantly on the move to find themselves in better circumstances, though I never knew just what those circumstances might be. What I did know without any doubt was that my father was the horse; my mother, driver and cart. Their comings and goings started well before their emigration to America and did not stop with their return to Ireland. For me, now, 'home' is nowhere, no place; it is, rather, a state of maximum connectedness. If you ask me if this is 'home' now, I'll tell you 'yes, at least for the time being'. I can't imagine myself living again as I did in Los Angeles, or giving up what I have created for myself here (with lots of help!), but certain things remain difficult, so I just keep building – one brick, one nail at a time.

Mo Sheana agus Mo Shinsir (All Who Came Before Me)

I'm sitting in Kruger's pub,
the past so suddenly with me
and the names, the names –
Maurice and Micheál (O'Sullivan and O'Guiheen),
Tomás, Peig, and Blaithín (who wrote of them) –

and the nameless, the dispossessed, the evacuees
who left their island homes.
Did they go, ice-floes of memory
among the scant belongings
they took to road or sea?
Were their burdens lightened
by the hint of smouldering turf
that clung to them?
Had they any notion then
they'd never know such wealth again?

EMMA SAVAGE

Beyond the Tide

Eoin scrunched up the dandelions and tossed them into the breach, their flight spurred on towards that mysterious landmass across the way. A craggy shape peeked out at him, past the mist, almost taunting him. They never talked much about that place over there.

For a time, he had been certain that they were alone in that whirlpool they called the ocean. But there were vast expanses beyond the horizon, places he could only dream of. He planted himself on the soil, watching as stray beams of light fought their way through the cloud.

The water lapped at the sand a small distance off, beckoning. Poseidon would have to wait; only a weak adventurer would seek help from a deity. Eoin had no need for such aid. For he was the hero who had expelled those pests from their patch a moon ago – yes, the hero who even uncovered the cave of jewels by the stream over yonder!

Yet his body was still too small to make the journey alone. They spoke sometimes of boatloads of people seeking out riches and dragons in other lands. His feet almost moved on their own to hop into the boats with the many, to lead them on an unending journey of wonder. Then again, he may be more successful if he waited until he was a little bigger.

But he didn't have time to waste.

'Oi, get over here. Your ma needs help.'

A few moments passed. Perhaps the dandelions didn't make it over the water after all.

He plucked a few more from the ground.

Then he got to his feet, sparing another glance at the briny deep. Someday he would traverse it, discovering the riches and rewards of that mysterious island. Its golden sunshine and eternal summer – the vast trappings of his spiralling castle – its promise twanged at his heart. There he wouldn't see his home's disrepair or feel the pang in his stomach. He needn't see the frail figures in their township nor hear the tales of the workhouses.

Yes – he'd have everything he could ever imagine. A new life and a wonderful world to explore. He just needed to get across the water.

REBECCA CRAWFORD

From Peru to Portaferry

Whilst we proceed on our way to our different occupations, may pleasant breezes fill your sails, to waft you speedily and safely on yours; and when again, you reach your native land (that ever beloved land!) – may it be in the enjoyment of good health and prosperity.

Letter from the passengers on board the *Asia* to Captain Henry Maxwell, *Belfast Newsletter,* 14 November 1853

There is nothing quite like standing on moss after a downpour. As your boots plunge into the marauding mess of flora, water leaps up around your heels, and the ground sighs beneath you. Warm and wet, it felt as if the entire world was cocooned around me. However, unlike the leaves stuck to my coat, these boots were foreign. Made from the hides of cows that had never grazed upon a drumlin.

My pleasure was diminished by the sensation of dampness. I examined my boot. There was a button-sized hole in the sole. The moss had sought me out. Green fingers curled up against my threadbare sock, like a dog against his master. Sighing, I realised it would have served me well to spare a few bob on another pair while I was in the colonies. Somehow, I had forgotten – after my time spent pacing up and down the sun-baked earth – how even on cloudless days the Irish season seeps into the soil.

My ill fortune began when I first joined the *Asia*. What I had assumed would be my initial steps towards fortune turned out to lead only to misery. A few days into the initial journey, I started to sweat. My body became a sticky mess and my stomach spun in circles, like a bird trapped in a cage. Running over to the edge of the deck, I vomited up three days' worth of food. The following afternoon, as I hung over the railings after another bout of sickness, a bottle was shoved in my face. I smiled weakly and took a swig. After a few seconds, my mouth was filled with bitter fizz, while a prickly spice danced up and down my throat.

'What the . . . ' I coughed into my hand. Couldn't tell if I was drinking it or it was drinking me.

'You've never had ginger ale?' The man grinned. 'My wife's own blend. I used to be a bit pale on deck myself, but this stuff keeps my head' – he patted his stomach – 'and everything else steady.'

Nodding, I slumped against the rail.

'Stay in the fresh air. Keep yourself busy.' He put his arm around my shoulder and walked me towards the stern. 'And stick where the floor's stable.' He removed something from his pocket and placed it in my hand. 'Eat some of these too.'

Frowning, I opened the paper bag. It was full of cubes of crystallised ginger. I glanced up to say something but the stranger was gone.

That afternoon I was finally able to do some work. My stomach rolled over with the waves on a few occasions but after I took some ginger the sickness ebbed away. Asking around the cabins, I found out the man's name. It was our very own captain. He was notorious for looking out for new bloods, they told me. And a pleasant man to the passengers, no matter the class. I cursed myself for being too sick to tell the captain from an ordinary sailor. He must have thought I was a disrespectful fool.

But, being who he was, Captain Maxwell was a busy man. I never had a chance to talk to him until after the *Asia* disembarked at Melbourne. Then it was just a quick thank-you and a tired smile from both of us. My words floated away on the sea breeze, tangling with those of our passengers, glad to have survived the trip.

What an adventure it was, too. We left England on the twenty-sixth of September and arrived in Australia on the thirtieth of December, ready to start 1855 with a bit of pomp and flourish. The *Asia* was a fine ship, with two decks and a comfortable eight feet between them. A copper-bottomed schooner from Belfast, the papers all over the North advertised our voyage with great excitement. We could carry between four and six hundred passengers, most of whom were Irish that we picked up in London. The previous season was more prosperous – we picked up five hundred and fifty when we were in Liverpool.

Captain Maxwell was an experienced man, having sailed the *Riverdale* only a few years before. Some of the crew were from the old ship. I couldn't imagine how they could stick being tossed around the seas for years on end. For me, this would be my first and last voyage across the world.

Our next port of call was Callao in Peru, to ship some cargo – things like crates of brandy and gin – then we were to head back to British waters. After the trek across the globe, it sounded easy. We'd all be home faster than you could shine your boots. But just off the Chincha Islands, our luck would turn sour.

The trouble started when I discovered a rat nibbling at my bootlaces. After some cursing and kicking, I scared the brute away. I looked around for Toby. The lazy beggar usually spent his mornings at the end of my bed. But there was nothing but a dishevelled blanket, plucked from overuse, lying there. Assuming he'd gotten bored and gone elsewhere, I began searching for my snuffbox. Then I spotted a ginger ear under the bed. Smirking, I grabbed Toby to wake him up but soon realised my mistake. He was as cold as fresh water.

After putting on my boots, I took the cat up onto the first deck. The men were busy at work, washing the floor and shifting boxes. Someone was playing a tin whistle, while a group – the O'Neill brothers – was singing along. Walking over to the edge, I said my goodbyes just as the final notes trembled in the air. After a nod at one of the fellows sweeping nearby, I tipped the fluffy corpse into the Pacific.

'There he is.' Captain Maxwell took a sip from his glass. 'Have you been well?'

'Thanks to you.' I nodded. 'Better than poor Toby.'

'Blast. Let's hope that's not some sort of omen, eh?'

Captain Maxwell peeked over the side, scowling. 'Toby was a bit of a nuisance. And our other cat has been lame ever since that barrel fell on her.' He sighed. 'Well, glad to see you're in better form, lad.' Captain Maxwell tapped the rail. 'Any more bother, come see me. I've a cure for everything – except homesickness.' He winked and raised his glass. 'That's what this is for.'

I did go to see him the following week. He was a good talker. Didn't look down at his men, like some might. With ears that jut out like a monkey's, mind as sharp as the cook's knife and a wicked sense of humour, Henry was a good man. But he hadn't the best foresight. Another captain might have bought some kittens when he was in the colonies, but Captain Henry thought our duo would manage. Nobody argued with him. After the incident with Toby, the mice trebled in number. Vermin skittered about on deck, like they'd bought themselves first-class tickets, and sang to us at night. It was a dreadful affair.

But bad luck always comes in threes, doesn't it?

I set down the bundle of daisies I'd been carrying. It all seemed so recent. The tricks our memories play on us make some days close and others a mile away. A sudden laugh exploded out of my mouth. If only he knew. A skivvy like me, getting sentimental. He'd call me an eejit, for sure. I could see the deep line across his forehead, the turn in the corner of his lips, as I'd hand him the bouquet.

My smile faded as I pictured Eleanor, dressed in black, with a toddler tugging at the hem of her dress. Where did she go, after the service? Her parents' cottage, probably, where the family would start planning a remarriage after a few months of hanging cloth over their mirrors.

I brushed my fingers across Captain Maxwell's name. It was strange. A man whose booming laugh used to fill the cabin was now nothing but a few words on a granite block. The mottled surface I stroked was nothing like the smooth-skinned, bright-eyed man who slept underneath it. I tickled the letters of his birth as though I could tease him back into existence with a flick of my fingertips.

But it was hopeless.

A year has passed since the incident on deck. We'd brought him up to see the sky. It was as blue as Indian sapphires. Or so we'd told him. But Captain Maxwell never took a man at his word. Stubborn to the end, he had to see it for himself. I protested, but after some thought I ended up getting permission from the first mate, who had taken on the role of captain after Henry started showing the first signs.

When we reached the deck Captain Maxwell told us that he was glad it was sunny. If it had been stormy it would have just made him think of home. I remember telling him that it was all right, that we'd be back in Ireland by the end of the month. He'd never have to worry about sunshine again. Captain Maxwell smiled and began to chuckle. But his laughs were distorted by a volley of coughs, which didn't subside until he spat blood into his handkerchief. Then we took him back to his bed.

And he never left it again.

We ended up putting him into a crate, after the youngest of the O'Neills found him in early June. We packed it full of salt and perfume and kept it in the corner of the hold. Normally, we'd give him an ocean burial, but our captain wouldn't have liked that. Before he passed on, Captain Maxwell asked us to ensure that he was buried back in his hometown of Portaferry under the same stone where his mother, father, Captain James Maxwell of the *Robert Ker* and brothers Hugh and Samuel rested. No matter what, he said, he had to go back home. He was born there. And he was going to be buried there.

So, while some of us dreamt of fields and clean beds on our return, Captain Maxwell's dreams were lost in the dark, smothered by the stench of musk.

'What do you smell now, eh?' I stood up and brushed the dirt off my trousers. 'Nothing. Not even the manure they've used in the field across the way.'

I turned to look over my shoulder. A crow was cawing. It was perched nearby, atop a crumbling stone wall. Catching sight of my stare, the bird croaked once before opening its wings. For some reason it made me think of the pooka. Captain Maxwell had told me about it, during one of our longs nights of drinking. A creature who liked to shift into an animal and lure men to their deaths. I watched the black shape as it flew away. I'd forgotten what it was like to stand under a sky as dull as the graves around me. I winced. It wasn't just grey. This was a horizon exactly the same shade as Captain Maxwell's face as we placed him in the crate.

A sky the colour of consumption.

GRÁINNE TOBIN

Security

for Jeff Collins

Where was it I read that after Chinese emperors
were long gone, knees still buckled at the sight
of a Party official, and it was all the poor
people could do to stop themselves kowtowing?

Remember dropping to the ground at a bang
from a car exhaust in some English high street,
showing opened bags in chainstore doorways,
checking all kerbs for unattended cars?

As infants' mouths turn to a fingertip,
we were hand-reared for spycam and scanner,
suspected, monitored, bad with our nerves,
arms held out in prayer or surrender.

Bread and Jam

Leaving for England the first time, your cabin trunk
arrived at your college a fortnight after you did.
Two weeks of startling men you passed, just by saying hello,
not knowing that you were a young woman, therefore
your small-town courtesies would be taken for seduction.
And once the trunk was unfastened, you saw what you had packed:
black skirts such as a nun might wear when habits were relaxed,
wrapped round six jars of your mother's gooseberry jam,
like the food left in coffins to keep the dead going.

Leaving for England years later to visit the grandparents
of your hybrid children with their transplanted father,
your car boot is searched at the docks for explosives and found instead
to contain several loaves of wheaten bread.
And here is what the searcher said.
They all pack bread. You can't get decent bread in England.

Going Home

They called their neighbours *the cockneys,*
and every summer gathered saved-up money
for the Holyhead boat, and then the drive
across the Bog of Allen, where every village
had its own song that the mother sang –
the main street is a row of trees
where the liars dwell as thick as thieves –
to sons and daughters wedged in the back seat,
looking sideways at green letterboxes with 'ER' painted over,
at the cream and emerald trim of post offices
whose signs said *Oifig an Phoist* in Gaelic Revival script,
small shops with bacon-slicers on the counter,
where they'd pop the crown cork off your mineral
and wheedle for details of seed, breed and generation,
to place you on the map of townlands and reputation,
family feuds, *where is it he is now,*
indexing the archives of the lost and the returned.

II

'The crystal clear air and stillness of west Mayo. . .'

from 'Leaving Ireland'
Kathy Ryder

MIKE McCORMACK

Six Snapshots of Emigration

I

Emigration is not so much a theme as a family- and community-shaping presence.

My family on both sides, from North and South Mayo, was shaped by it. It sent sons and daughters to England and America in the sixties, seventies and eighties – navvies and miners and tattie-hokers and factory workers. My father worked on buildings in London, gold mines in Canada and tunnels in New York. My mother was a tattie-hoker who came down from Scotland to London to work in factories and hospitals. To this day it gives me pause to think that my siblings and I are just one generation down from migrant workers. I saw the light of day in Holloway in 1965 and I spent the first four years of my life there.

So, when asked, I didn't need much coaxing to accept the task of steering an exploration into the meaning and experience of emigration. Here was an opportunity to enquire into an aspect of my own past which was foundational but also taken for granted, and ultimately something I was not at all sure I understood. Here was an opportunity to take a look at an unexplored aspect of myself.

Around a dozen of us met on six consecutive Friday afternoons in April and May of 2015; the Linenhall Arts Centre in Castlebar provided a room in which we could conduct our enquiries and discussions. Two-thirds were women, and the age profile was middle-aged and upward. Our motives for being there varied. Some wanted to record family histories; some wanted to pay tribute to courageous ancestors; some wanted to give narrative shape to people whose lives were little more than family folklore. People were enthusiastic but clear-eyed; they acknowledged the theme as large and rich but also as potentially difficult. Who knew what sediment it might stir up?

II

In both parts of Mayo where my family comes from emigration is such an integral part of the community that people no longer wonder at it. People marry and have families but it is inevitable that the majority of children will leave. People may be sorrowful about its existence but they are not astonished by it any more.

We had our Leaving Cert class reunion a couple of years ago. People turned up whom I had not seen in over twenty years. Sitting around and talking during the night, we calculated that three-quarters of our class had emigrated to either America or England, part of that tidal wave which left in the mid-eighties. To this day it is noticeable that there is a hole in the demographics of the broad catchment area around Louisburgh, a shortage of men and women in early middle age.

Those were the grim years for my generation, the eighties. Thirty years later I can still recall hitching a lift with a local man who had just left his daughter to the boat that same week. A big strong farmer behind the wheel of his Volkswagen, choked up with emotion not just for himself but for his whole village. 'Once the youth are gone, it tears the heart out of a community,' he said. His daughter had gone to London, one of that generation who navigated the city by way of the Mean Fiddler, the Archway Tavern, the music of the Pogues – all the rallying points and anthems of my generation's exodus.

III

So we delved into our stories of families scattered to America and England. We dug up tales of separation and loneliness, tales of families who thrived economically without ever fully making a home in their new countries, of families who were haunted by aunts and uncles who down the years had become ghost presences.

One of the men in the class raised an intriguing question: on balance, was the experience of emigration kinder to women than it was to men? Did they adapt to it better? Were they more comfortable with the whole fact of exile? He cited experiences in his own family of women who, after years in England, had returned to Ireland, sometimes against their will but following husbands who, for one reason or another, could not or would not settle in Britain. Some of these women brought with them an anger at having been forced to leave the more ordered and cleaner life of opportunity and material comfort in London to return to the harsher circumstances of rural Ireland. It would take some of them years to put this disappointment and anger behind them.

When this theme was raised there were several nods of affirmation around the table, not just among the women but among the men also. In this context, one of the most telling pieces in Liam Harte's anthology of emigrant writing from Britain is from Elaine Crowley's *Technical Virgins*. In it, she memorably recalls how, after her spell in the British Army during the Second World War, she remembered the physical squalor she would return to in the Dublin of the 1940s. For Crowley, England had become a sunlit place of ironed sheets and clean knickers and domestic order. When her contract with the Auxiliary Territorial Service was at an end she signed up immediately for another term rather than return home.

One of our contributors recalled her mother locking up the home place in Achill to move her young family to London. Summers would be spent returning to the farm cottage, their dog running down the road to meet them. Her mother would recall the decision to leave as the most difficult she had ever made, but also the best. Her courage was rewarded with a better life for her and her family.

Are men more susceptible to the sentimental draw to home? Does the savage love his native shore that much? I remember a man telling me his own reasons for returning home. He sounded baffled by his own feelings. 'I was doing well in London,' he said, 'plenty of work and money, a nice house, marriage and kids, the whole lot. But,' he shook his head, 'you're a stranger wherever you go. It's not home.'

IV

I wonder if there is not something to be celebrated in the culture of emigration. I don't mean emigrant culture as it is nurtured in those formal gatherings or festivities or showcases, nor in the songs or the stories or the exhibitions. I mean the act of leaving itself, and the way it has turned our gaze outward on the world, how it has readied us forever to take that first step abroad.

Any consideration of emigration is always shadowed by loss and separation and displacement. Present also is that national shame of a state failing to provide for its own people. Those are the leitmotifs. But several of our participants spoke fondly of going abroad to find their better selves. Education and employment and opportunity were mentioned but so too was the adventure of finding yourself in a foreign place and being forced to make your own way, stand on your own two feet, the whole anxious freedom of having choices to make.

Would it not be wise to find some way of celebrating this, giving it its proper due and embracing that intrepid part of ourselves? Could we not acknowledge the fact that this is who we are – a people who not only stay at home but also often go elsewhere to make our lives? Wouldn't such an acknowledgement and celebration go some way towards a fuller and more nuanced account of ourselves?

V

The separate villages my mother and father came from were tiny costal settlements, both windswept and exposed, and both situated at the ends of roads which ended up in the sea. But small as they were, these villages had an imaginative extension well beyond their narrow boundaries. Family members in

America and England expanded the imaginative scope of these communities to Kilburn High Road, to Boston suburbs, to bothies in Scotland. These small villages had much broader horizons than their immediate skylines. I wonder did this kind of psychic reach make us a more intrepid and inquisitive people? Did it make us spiritually hardier and more adaptable than we might have been? Is there any way of measuring this, any narrative technique which would allow us to see what worth it might have?

VI

Our explorations took place in an atmosphere of courtesy and generosity. The willingness to read and listen to each other's stories and to provide helpful criticism was a constant pleasure; so too the readiness to share experiences which were frequently sad and fragile. Time and again I was struck by how people were able to confirm and augment each other's memories. Many participants, for instance, had vivid memories of parcels and packages coming from America and London with clothes and books. I had known of the excitement and the economic boost which these packages brought with them; what I did not know was how those same packages were also a shameful badge of poverty and that their presence brought with them a measure of embarrassment which lingers to this day.

We have the statistical accounts and we have the sociological surveys. We have the predictable media cameos. To this day no Christmas TV schedule is complete without cameramen and reporters being deployed to national and regional airports to record our emigrants returning home to tearful families; the same reporters will be redeployed to the same spot in the first week of the new year to witness their leaving once more. These are the necessary but well-established public moments of emigration; they keep the phenomenon in our mind's eye. But these pieces – these poems, fictions and fragments of autobiography – attempt a different telling. Here is the beginning of that fuller account which seeks to explore how emigration continues to shape our hearts and our minds, how it has woven our souls.

My heartfelt thanks to all who participated.

BERNADETTE MEE-KEAVENEY

Annie's Story

I will never know the mind of the emigrant. I never emigrated but six of my seven siblings and many of my aunts and uncles did.

My mother grew up in Cortoon – Grace Kelly country – near Newport, County Mayo. Because her father brought some produce to the weekly market, they were known as 'Farmer Geraghtys', to differentiate them from other Geraghty families, which were variously known as 'Pottys', 'Yanks' and 'Giants'. In big families there are always 'pals', and though my mother had a twin sister, her other dear friend was her sister Annie. On Sunday their big treat was for one of them to carry their mother's prayer book in to Mass in Newport and the other to carry it home.

Annie was born on 17 February 1905, and when she married, as a young woman, she hoped to settle down locally. Sadly, her young husband, Sonny Cawley, died after only a year of marriage. Annie was forced to leave her husband's farm, and that's when she joined her brothers, Michael and Richard, in Chicago.

As youngsters, we were always mad to get the 'parcel from America' and have some of the check 'Margaret O'Brien' dresses we had seen on the child star of that name at the cinema. We also looked with envy at the parcels our neighbours received. Sadly, as it turned out, our American cousins were worse off than ourselves. When Annie returned to Ireland in 1961 – her first visit in forty years – she walked with the aid of two huge crutches, her infirmity gained from waiting in the snow for two different buses to take her to her job as carer to an old woman. Annie told my mother that she had pretended to be a nurse. I think she suffered enough for her lie. It seems that her Swedish husband had left her and their three little girls, and Annie was forced to find an income however she could.

When she came on that holiday she stayed with us for three months, while one of her daughters went to do a grand tour of Europe. I fondly remember herself and my dear mother having long chats about bygone days. She brought back from America their own mother's shawl, which had been sent to her by her brothers in Newport. I'm happy to say that the shawl is still in my possession.

Sheila A. McHugh

Only the Danger of the Poor Can Widen the Vision of the Rulers

I sat mesmerised on the low three-legged stool by the fire listening to the two older men talk of events in Achill, Donegal and Scotland, and at the Front. It was 1918, four years since we had returned to Achill from Dublin.

Both men were in Dublin in the lead up to, and during, the great Lockout of 1913. My father, the older of the two, had been a member of the Dublin Metropolitan Police and had taken 'early retirement', by choice or otherwise, on a pension of ten shillings a year. The other man was Peadar O'Donnell, a trainee teacher in St Patrick's College, Drumcondra at the time.

'What is the Front?' I asked, interrupting their flow of conversation.

I knew where Donegal and Scotland were from the big map hanging on the hook, high up on the wall in the master's room.

'The Front is where the Great War is taking place,' O'Donnell said, 'but we have our own war going on here at home.'

'What is the Great War?' I asked. 'Will we be fighting here too?'

'Will ye shush, lad,' my father intervened. 'You're too young to be listening. Go out and play.'

'No,' said O'Donnell to my father. 'If he is curious enough to ask, then it is better to expand on that curiosity.'

'Our war is different,' he said. 'Our war is against poverty and small thinking; hopefully no one will get killed, not like the Great War, where thousands of men, including many of our own, are being killed at the Front.'

My mind shifted to an eight-year-old's concept of war, but still with one ear cocked to the continuing conversation between the two men.

They talked about tattie-hokers, and going to Scotland, and gaffers. I knew what they were talking about. I had seen different groups of people gather in early springtime – some children I knew among them – and when I asked where they were going, my mother told me they were going to Scotland to pick potatoes. 'Would the children be picking potatoes too?' I asked. 'Yes, the children would be helping too,' she said.

O'Donnell talked about setting up a union for the workers from Donegal and Achill. My father listened attentively.

'How are you going to go about doing that?' he asked.

'What's a union?' I piped in.

'Will you shush, lad!' my father said with annoyance.

Ignoring him, O'Donnell said, 'It's where workers come together to fight for their rights.'

'What do you mean "fight for their rights"? What are "rights"?' I asked.

'Rights are what people are entitled to, like a fair wage for the work they do, and basic living conditions, like a clean and safe place to live, to sleep and to cook one's food,' O'Donnell said.

I shifted on the stool; I kinda knew what he meant.

'When people stand together, they are stronger,' he said. 'It's like when you are together with your friends, you do things you wouldn't do on your own. Am I right?'

I nodded my head.

The next day the three of us went in O'Donnell's car to Dooega to a meeting in the village school to form a union. There was a lot of serious talk about what a union was and different people asked questions about whether the gaffers and the farmers and the potato merchants in Scotland would listen.

'Sure, who are we anyway?' someone asked.

Another said, 'We have to borrow from the shopkeeper for the fare over, and already owe them what was on the slate.'

'Sure, who is going to listen to us?' another said.

A man stood up and said, 'We don't have enough to feed our families and ye're asking us not to go to Scotland because of some Bolshie idea that ye can stand up against the gangers over there.'

A woman spoke up. 'They don't care about us as long as they get the work done. They know we don't have a choice. We sleep in the bothies after they put the cows out to graze, and often we have to clean the cow dung out before we can set up our bedding. Bags they give us, that we have to fill with straw ourselves, that's all they give us to sleep on, and a thin blanket. They don't even give us a clean place to store the food and often we have to cook out in the open. Now, can ye do something about that?'

A clap went up in the room.

I saw O'Donnell stand up. He cleared his throat and said, 'If people would stand together they would have a stronger voice and be able to demand better conditions from the gaffers and the merchants in Scotland.'

My father was talking to another man. There was much shaking of their heads. Then the other man spoke.

'I recommend,' he said, 'that a labour group be set up from this meeting and that we affiliate to the Irish Transport and General Workers' Union in Dublin.'

There was much murmuring in the hall. Then my father raised his hand and, looking at O'Donnell, said, 'I second that, on condition that the workers in Donegal do the same thing.' Then there was more clapping and O'Donnell said that he would be meeting the Donegal workers at the weekend. Coming home in the car, I asked if they had made a union.

Over the following months and years, I read in the *Mayo News* about the effects this meeting and the union had on the workers. The workers were kept from going to Scotland as a means of putting pressure on the potato merchants for better pay and living conditions. At first, the merchants and gaffers knew that the workers needed to go to Scotland, and didn't give in to their demands. It was a harder than usual time for the workers and their families; they needed the money they earned in Scotland to pay off their debts and have something left over to see them through the remainder of the year. The hope they had put in the union was beginning to wane. My father said that the gaffers were able to put pressure on them here at home, and the workers were afraid that they would not have any work in Scotland. O'Donnell kept in touch with the local organisers, and between them they were able to get better pay for the workers, though the living conditions did not improve.

There was so much going on: civil war had broken out and we were fighting among ourselves. O'Donnell had written to my father saying that he had left his work with the unions to become a full-time active member of the IRA. 'It is a bigger cause,' he said. He asked for me, and how I was doing in school.

There was something about the man that I liked. We didn't hear from him for a while; my father said he was busy fighting the Blueshirts. Different men would come and stay with us for a night or two. My mother would feed them, but they made her nervous. She was afraid that the Black and Tans would come. I had been told to say I didn't know anything, though everyone knew something.

After the civil war and the land annuity campaign, O'Donnell returned to Achill for a rest, and to write. I was full of curiosity about the civil war and what he did. I would join him on his walk through the village; often we would be joined by young fellas from the area. A couple of times a week he would meet a group of us secretly at the old coastguard station and talk to us about the cause of Irish freedom. He taught us how to use a weapon and how to move about without being noticed. As a lesson on how to deal with fear, he told us about his experience of being put in prison.

'Fear,' he told us, 'is the beginning of wisdom. But fear without faith in yourself is the end of wisdom. You'll find yourself scurrying down a dark hole. So,' he said, looking around at each of us, 'stop and ask yourself if you have ever been afraid before, and how did you shake yourself out of it.'

Walking back to the house together one evening, I asked him how he got to know so much. He stopped and was quiet for a moment, then said, 'I have learned some things from books, but most of my learning is from people in places like Achill and the Donegal islands. If only the people here knew their worth,' he said, 'you could change the world.'

News had come through of a drowning tragedy off Arranmore Island in Donegal. Twenty people, most of them islanders coming home from Scotland, drowned. The O'Donnells headed back up there to be with the people.

In the spring of 1936 I went to work on a farm in England. Accommodation on the farms in England was not much better than that in Scotland: rats, mice and fleas were constant bedding companions. You shook DDT all around the place where you were sleeping; it did keep the rats and mice away.

I was back home in September 1937 when more bad news arrived. This time it was our own island, our own people. Ten young Achill men were burned to death in a bothy fire in Kirkintilloch. I wrote to O'Donnell. There was a fire burning in me, an anger that I needed to entrust to someone I thought would understand. He wrote back, urging patience and caution. 'I too am angry at the failure to attain better conditions, both at home and in Scotland for the migrant workers. We must retreat and regroup in our thinking. The island folk had failed because they were not dangerous enough. Only the danger of the poor can widen the vision of the rulers.'

He invited me to go to Donegal after the funerals were over. I wanted to do something but didn't know where to start; I knew I didn't have the experience. In the O'Donnell home we talked long into the night. Most of the time he was trying to anchor me in my thinking, advising me on the importance of planning and of having a strategy to follow.

In June 1938 O'Donnell sent me a telegram from Girvan in Scotland. 'Would you take position as organiser of Scottish Farm Servants' Union, migratory section? If so, wire me in Dublin and come here Saturday with motorbike.' He ended by saying, 'Strongly recommend acceptance.' When O'Donnell said 'strongly recommend acceptance' he did not expect to receive 'no' for an answer.

So off I went to Dublin on my motorbike, and from there to Scotland with a list of recommendations, do's and don'ts, from O'Donnell. In addition to trying to enrol the workers in the union and organise collectors of union dues from within each squad, I inspected the accommodation and bothies where the workers stayed and reported those that did not meet requirements to the Scottish Farm Workers' Union.

There was a core of workers who saw the worth of being part of a union: they were mostly women. Women were at the forefront of efforts to obtain better conditions, but as O'Donnell had warned me, they did not get the support of the men. 'The men hated the work: the women loathed it,' he explained. 'The heaviest burden of this world fell on the women.'

It wasn't easy work, but I had the continued support of O'Donnell and Duncan of the Scottish Farm Workers' Union. As Duncan said, there has been 'too much of the stick method in Ireland. People who are accustomed to being driven will not act on their own initiative.'

This was not easy to hear. But O'Donnell's words rang in my ears. 'Sit with it, lad, and learn from it.' Other words of his came to me too. 'For the curse of their countryside is that every word heard rising out of it, and every mind seen reaching out of it, is stricken with littleness.'

I began to see that people who are continuously challenged by conditions imposed by history and landscape are shown to be tough, resilient and creative in surviving amid the limitations of their environment. As O'Donnell would be wont to say, the people of Achill and Arranmore are learning that life is not just about survival. People still remain tough, alive, vital with the power of imaginative co-operation and its odd moments of inspiration.

I too was learning from O'Donnell about the power of imaginative co-operation, a trait he had already seen, mostly in the women of the islands. It was through the women that he saw the possibility of change happening. I had seen the courage, the resilience and most of all the good humour of the women in Scotland, amid terrible conditions. These women saw beyond their conditions; they had a vision of a better life for themselves and their children.

Is this what O'Donnell meant by the danger of the poor widening the vision of the rulers?

GER REIDY

Maybe It's Because I'm a Londoner

There were two of us for the eighty acres when I met Bridgie. She changed everything. I was on the road at the time with the threshing machine, using the reaper and binder too – all set up, I thought. The brother got a job in the bacon factory in Castlebar, office boy; never wanted the land anyway, but it didn't turn out that way.

When the mother saw me that evening after Johnny Quinn's funeral with Bridgie going across Market Square, I knew there would be consequences. That night after the dance in the Gaiety they were both waiting up for me on either side of the fire, the old fella silent, she speaking into a space as if someone had a terminal disease. It was the land or Bridgie. I had a month to decide.

The brother was afraid to say anything. That month went by as if I was carrying some invisible weight. Every day I hoped that an answer would present itself but confusion swirled in my brain. I spent every evening with Bridgie as if I was on death row. Maybe I was hoping she would become ordinary and some sense would dismiss her so I could restore my old life, but I couldn't get enough of her. My parents were cheerful, as if nothing was happening. I fed the sheaves into the thresher like a blind man. I wasn't safe to be around. The men couldn't understand what was happening.

On the last evening I kissed her at the handball alley and finally knew that the price had to be paid. I couldn't tell her; I couldn't tell anyone the torture I was going through. When I went home I looked at the machinery and knew too that it was part of me and that I would have to bring it with me to wherever I was going.

The following morning I was up before dawn on the road, the lads leading the horse and driving the machinery down the road. I stopped at the house as I was passing. My mother was there, holding a pitchfork. I waved one last time but she turned around and went into the turf shed.

John Keane came out of his low cottage pulling his braces over his shoulders and grabbed a hold of the mare. What are you at, William? Don't let them do this to you. John was a decent man who made the best of his twenty-three acres of rushes. Stop, he kept saying, what will the parish do without you? My old fella and John spent many a Sunday shooting rabbits. He pleaded with me the way my father should have, before we shook hands and turned away.

We had to make for the boat after I sold the horses. There was a commotion at the crossroads as we were passing through with the machinery. An old woman proclaimed in a low voice that the same name would never last two generations in a row in that house. There was big work in Yorkshire, where me and Bridgie would live with my Uncle Leslie until we got our own place.

The boat was rough. Bridgie couldn't stand the smell of the cattle coming from below. It was the first storm of the winter and some fine Hereford bullocks were crushed. They took the cattle off before us for some reason. It was sad to see them swinging the dead animals onto the quays in Birkenhead. We stayed in Liverpool, our first night together as a free couple. Everyone assumed we were married. It felt right.

Our machinery took a week to get to Yorkshire but there was still some threshing to be done. I helped Leslie with his tillage farm that autumn, sowing the winter wheat. He was good to us. I think he was lonely since his wife Charlotte died. We weren't used to the winters in Yorkshire, the cold wind off the North Sea; and the snow cut us off for weeks in February. We stayed two years with him before we rented our own place. Two boys and two girls, Bridgie wanted. Then the war came. We would have made money if we'd stayed in Yorkshire but Bridgie wanted to be with her aunt in London to help her with the shop. What am I going to do in London? I demanded. The O'Malleys will look after us. They always look after their own – not like your crowd, Bridgie laughed. I parked up the machinery in Leslie's place that winter, assuming the war would be over in a few months, not knowing that I'd never see Yorkshire again.

When everyone else was leaving London, we were moving in. I got a job in a brewery pub near Elephant and Castle, up at five to clean the pipes, the Irish boys demanding drink at eight. The money came in. Soon I was running my own place. Then one night it happened. They told me that I was the only one to walk out alive, pulled me from under a pile of red bricks. Bridgie was gone. On the front of the *Evening Press* in Ireland was our wedding photograph. I had no choice but to keep going. The O'Malleys were good to me. I moved in with her aunt over the shop until I got another pub. The brewery were good too. I had to develop a limp to avoid the draft and I bought a taxi plate to get petrol.

Almost every night the siren went off. Sleeping in the tube station, it was sad to see the children crouching under old coats beside their parents, emerging at dawn to find their homes blown away. I missed Bridgie something awful that first year. There was nothing for it except to keep my mind off her with work. Living over the pub alone was too much sometimes and the odd night I brought a girl upstairs. We never got up to much: I think it was the company I craved. Soon I was raking in the money, bought myself nice clothes, became chairman of the local vintners' association. Then I met Doris, my Doris.

After the war the place flooded with big lonely Irish men. They stayed too long in the pubs, rolls of cash falling out of their pockets, talking about Belmullet or Killybegs, couldn't face the bedsit alone. We gave them the sub midweek; the women chatting them up on Fridays relieved them of a few bob too. I had three pubs going then. Me and Doris; they were good years. Doris couldn't have kids but that was fine, I loved her, anything my Doris wanted she got. We always took Sundays off, got someone in. Doris always said if we couldn't do that, it wasn't worth it.

Every few years me and Doris went back to Ireland to see the brother, his wife and three kids, splashed a few bob and met the locals in the Central Hotel. He made a go of the land and kept his job in the factory. He was the man I could never be. I often thanked God for the day I went down the road with the threshing machine and poor John Keane trying to stop me. I suppose it's Bridgie I should thank. I could never go back. I was a Cockney now, and to think that I could be walking cattle to a fair seemed another world – afraid of the priest and waiting for the rain to stop.

The brother and I got on well now, a quiet, responsible man, built a new house. I envied him sometimes, well respected in the community, kids going to university. The locals liked the Bentley, it caused a stir, especially outside the village church, with forty black bikes around it. It wasn't the pubs that bought it, though, it was the gold I brought in to Ireland. I never told Doris about it.

Anyway, we went back for the funerals, the mother a brain tumour in '57, the old fella Parkinson's in '63. We had big money them years but the horses were my poison. I passed this fella once coming home from Westport with a jute bag in the trailer being pulled by a Ferguson 35. Is them the wet or the dry batteries? I enquired, to make conversation. Ah, is that the ways you are? he ridiculed me. That is the new black and white TV I'm renting for the Sonny Liston-Cassius Clay fight. Half the parish are coming to my place tonight, and you're welcome. We went. Clay had his man down fairly quick, bottles of porter everywhere. They were generous, I'll give them that, but there was always an angle, jobs with the subcontractors or work in the pubs. I looked after them, fed them too – sure they drank it away in my place.

Kilmeena Lass was the name of my horse in Ascot. She fell at the last and had to be put down. All the lads had big money on her: it was a turning point. Drink, well you can only take so much, but with the nags, it's a disease. By '71 we were broke again, me outside the bar, my own best customer. Doris dumped me; she was right. Kicked the habit, got tired of feeling sorry for myself. We were back together again in '73, Deptford this time, small place just off the high street.

I started going to church again. Doris was trying to keep me on the straight and narrow: anything was better than the hell we had been through. I was beginning to be grateful now for simple things; the money didn't matter as much any more. It began to bother me, all the old men with nowhere to go, especially the retired ones with no pension. At weekends they seemed to be everywhere when me and Doris went for a walk. Anyway, all these men almost lived in our pub and we made it again. We fed them too, the ones who couldn't go home, and

Father Luke buried them in the purple cardboard coffins, nobody to be found belonging to them. Bought Doris mink coats, determined I was to look after her this time, but she had to slow down, with the pacemaker and the hip. We had it good until the blacks moved in, stabbed a guy one night. That closed the place and we were too old to start over. I got a basement flat in Hughes Field estate surrounded by Jamaicans. The kids were lovely but we had to put grilles on the windows. We did venture out every Saturday night to the Harp of Erin in the mini-cab and to St John's Community Hall for the bingo on Wednesdays.

I couldn't afford to go home any more but a young fella came over last year, the brother's youngest son, an engineer he was, I think. Anyway, he brought us out. It was a long time since we were in the city for a night. I had this terrible feeling going across London Bridge that I'd never see it again. I was gaping out the taxi window as if I had just come off the boat at Holyhead but something told me that I was on a farewell tour. I broke into 'Maybe It's Because I'm a Londoner' before the melancholy hit and a few tears leaked out, but I kept smiling for Doris. I gave the young fella a mink coat from the old times; Doris wouldn't mind.

He left me off at a nightclub where I was collecting glasses; on the way to the airport he was. I clasped his hand tightly and said goodbye. Before that I looked at him in the eye. Get yourself a steady job, I said, a nice girl, live a different life to what you see here. I know there's big money on the buildings but I've seen them, the way they end up. Try the County Council or the Civil Service, I said, because I knew that's what the brother would have wanted me to say. It was the least I could do for the brother to try and keep his only son on the land, even though I didn't believe what I was saying. Maybe I wanted the old place to be kept in the family after all. Since the day I left I wanted to see the house burned down and the land sold off, but Father Luke persuaded me when I got sick to let things go. Maybe I was forgiving the mother in some strange way after all these years. Sometimes parents are cruel to protect their own. It goes back to the Famine, Father Luke used to say.

Anyway, the young fella dismissed me as if he would see me again. I gave him grandfather's old pocket watch. Mind your old fella, I said as I let his hand go. He's a better man than I could ever be. My gaze followed him as his taxi faded into the night traffic.

Kathy Ryder

Leaving Ireland

Like so many households in the west of Ireland, the emigration boat took every member of my family and my mother's family before us away from Ireland in search of work and a new life, in either England or America.

We lived in a valley, which meant that every leaving involved walking over a small bridge, up a steep hill, on top of which grew a hollybush – the final point of goodbye – and the white waving handkerchief slowly disappearing from sight. I had watched this ritual so many times, particularly the departures of my father, who had worked away from home for my entire childhood, and more recently my older sisters too. Now my hour had come; I was going to be the one with the handkerchief.

It all happened so quickly, after I returned from a month in the Gaeltacht. My mother thought it a good idea for me to accompany Teresa, an older sister, to Pinner in Middlesex. Teresa was home on her annual fortnight's holiday, a week of which was already over. I was happy to go; in fact, quite excited by the prospect of it all, as I absolutely hated school and the cruel regime it was then. My parents had met, married and lived in England for eight years in the 1930s and my mother especially had always spoken very fondly of her time there. We had family and friends in the Pinner area who visited us most summers. I looked forward to knowing them better and to having the same sort of nice clothes.

I imagine my mother thought I'd be better out of the way, while she and Bridget, another older sister, packed up our life on our small farm in west Mayo. During that summer, my mother sold off the cattle and basically anything that was saleable, except our house and farm. We gave our dog Randy to a neighbour who lived a mile away; he was named after a showband singer my sister had a crush on. For many years afterwards, within a day of us returning home on holiday, Randy would walk across the hill, come right in and lie under the table. The rattle of the enamel breadbin lid still caused him to jump to his feet. Back then, bread and scraps were a dog's normal diet.

I had very little time to dwell on how final a move this was. I said goodbye to friends, my mother, younger brother and sister, the kind lady who ran the local shop, and the dog. I knew I would see my family in London in about six weeks, so I remember looking more forward than back as I left the home where I was born and from which I had never ventured further than twenty miles. The ten o'clock bus took us to Westport, from where we went by train to Dublin's

Westland Row, then took the boat train to Dún Laoghaire, the boat to Holyhead and on to London's Euston Station, where we were jolted from sleep in the early hours of the following morning.

My first impressions were not good. There were dark dirty buildings with smoke everywhere, not just from the arriving and departing trains, but also from factories and domestic dwellings, where at that time coal provided the main source of heat, energy and stuffy smells – not at all like the familiar smell of turf smoke. Everything seemed to be dirty, grey, grim even. Porters shuffling around in dark clothes, noisy crowds all around. This whole scene couldn't have been more of a contrast to the wide open spaces, the crystal clear air and stillness of west Mayo.

Finally, we arrived at the large three-bedroom flat my father had rented in Pinner. I have no idea where my ideas of grandeur came from, but I wasn't overly impressed. It was quite luxurious relative to what I'd just left, but not nearly as fancy as I had hoped. My father was there to greet me and while it was nice to see him, as far as I was concerned, although only just fifteen, I had now stepped into adulthood and the father I had only ever seen for two short holiday breaks each year was not about to tell me what I could and couldn't do.

There was one incident before my mother arrived in England, when he forbade me to go to the dance that my much older sisters were going to. He wanted me to come with him to visit Mary, another married sister, but I told him I'd stay home. When I got him gone, I got ready for the dance, put a couple of pillows longways in the bed and pulled a chair up against the door, leaving just enough room for him to peek in. He was in bed by the time we got back and he never did discover that I had been to that dance. That adventure was the beginning of freedom and an introduction to the England that I quickly grew to know and love. I found English people to be kind and encouraging, with never a thought that I might get a big head if they praised me – what a difference from the school regime I had left behind.

*

The decision to leave Ireland happened when my mother's sister Rose came from New York to visit in 1960. My grandfather had died in 1945 and my grandmother in 1955, so there were no caretaking obligations for my mother. Aunt Rose wasn't shy in letting us hear her viewpoint. She reminded my mother that apart from the first couple of years in England, the family had never lived together and that the children see their father as a visitor. My three older sisters had all left to work in England at eighteen years of age. The remaining three would most likely do the same and within a few more years my mother would be alone, keeping land, tending cattle and maintaining the house for everyone to come on holiday to once a year, while my father still worked in Dublin.

Norah, my mother, on being reminded of her circumstances, remembered how she had loved England. Even after her father died, she had tried to persuade her mother to go back to Oxfordshire, where they had lived during the first year of the war. It was a nice country place; she felt sure she'd be happy there. Another fifteen years had passed since then; her roots in Ireland had grown deeper. She had survived the hardship of the early years, having and taking care of babies and young children and nursing her aging and dying parents alone. But she was young and strong then, a grass widow, like so many women.

She knew what Rose was saying to be true and, further influenced by a short holiday in Harrow with Aunt Rose, the idea of leaving became firmly planted. When my father came home that Christmas, she told him that we would all pack up home in Mayo and move to Harrow. In February 1961 he left his job with the Board of Works in Dublin. On arrival in England, he quickly got a job with an engineering company, Glacier Bearings, doing similar work to what he had been doing in Dublin. He remained there for the rest of his working life.

In May 1962, just eight months after we arrived in Pinner, a lovely four-bedroom house in Hindes Road, Harrow was settled on, the same road on which my mother had, in her single years, worked as a cook in a nursing home. The bulk of the deposit for this house came from the sale of cattle and other belongings in Ireland. Its price was £3,250; my father's extra offer of £50 was what clinched the deal. It remained our home for thirty-one years and the gathering place for many Irish friends who lived in bedsits and lodgings.

During the process of trying to find the right house we had telephone calls from estate agents. On the first of these occasions after my mother arrived, she answered the phone and the agent asked to speak to my father. She returned the phone to the cradle and went to call him, not realising she had cut the agent off. Hard to believe now, but it probably was the first time my mother had ever answered a telephone. The agent phoned back a little later and asked to speak to a *responsible* person.

In the years that followed our move to England my mother often said that it was the hardest thing she had ever done in her life, to close the house, put up the shutters and walk away with her children. She also said it was the best thing she ever did. It was the 28th of September 1961. The following morning they arrived in Pinner, on the tenth birthday of my youngest sister Noreen and the thirteenth birthday of my brother Johnny. They had brought with them the meagre amount of clothes they possessed and a Pye radio, which my mother had bought in 1959.

My mother, exhausted from the whole experience, talked as if to herself about the leaving. 'They all came to visit the night before we left. Rose Ann, Tilly, Katie, Margaret, all the neighbours and cousins – it was like a wake. I told them we'd be back every summer for the length of the school holidays and we will. They kept turning around and shining the flash lamps back at me as they walked out the hill; that was breaking my heart! Eventually they went out of sight at the hollybush. I slept little, up early to put up the shutters and clear every bit of food, leave the trunk of bed clothes back to Martin's to put behind the fire in the room above, stand the mattresses on end – so much to think of. Tom O'Boyle arrived with his Volkswagen van to bring us to the early train. He was upset too; we were always great friends, both him and his people before him. I keep thinking of the house now, dark and lonely after all the years. It's forty years since my father finished it and I slept there the first night. And poor Martin too, the last person in that valley, how lonely he will find our house compared to what he's used to. No one there to pass a friendly word with, or offer him a cup of tea, on his comings and goings to the shop or the bus.'

It took Noreen at least a year to settle and I don't think I fully understood the extent of her grief back then. Fifty-two years later, she wrote a piece for a commemoration booklet I produced for our primary school reunion in 2013. I was quite taken aback by what she wrote:

> What I recall vividly is the excitement I felt on those rare occasions when we rounded Garvey's corner and the school door was closed. The happiness was almost always short-lived; the master or missus would appear out of nowhere and the school day would begin. The day before my tenth birthday I emigrated with my family to England, where a new world would eventually open up for us. On many occasions thereafter I would have given anything to have seen the welcoming sight of Rossgalive School door open and been able to walk through and enjoy the comfort and familiarity of my lovely classmates and teachers. While my recollection of those beautiful years is sparse, I know there was such a rich sense of community and genuine care for each other. It was a truly special time.

My family returned to our old home every summer for extended holidays and we all cried enough when we were leaving. I myself have been living back in Mayo for more than thirty years now, but I still have a great grá and gratitude for England – for the opportunities I was given, the friends I made, the kindness I received – and I always feel a sense of homecoming on my regular visits there.

ANN MORAN

Traversing the Shiny Openness

Mam and Dad drove me to Knock
we were quiet, I think
I didn't get it

All I was thinking of
was seeing Steve
he had gone on
before me

We sat in the bar
had a coffee, I think
Mam handed me a note
'Read it on the plane'

Went into Departures
said goodbye
they were gone
didn't get it yet

On the plane
I sat, feeling nothing
in the air
I opened the note

From my mother
saying nice things
wishing me luck
saying farewell

Tears welled
I felt it then
folded it up
put it away

Touched down at
Luton Airport (oooowieooo!)
like the song
traversed the shiny openness

With my suitcase
and black shawl
I spotted a
lone man
in a Crombie coat
arms outstretched

The Woman who Walked into Doors: A Snapshot from a Memoir

ZZZZZZ

Angela was snoring loudly, kinda snorting.

Her long blonde hair draped over her shoulder, her head turned to one side. She always looked more attractive from the back. Her tall slender figure, her hair perfectly straightened, her manicured nails. She really looked gorgeous from the back. Her face was a disappointment, though. It was a bit big and she wasn't that pretty. But she was nice to me. A glass of white wine, Petit Chablis, half full, was positioned to her eleven o'clock and a twenty pack of Dunhill was left strewn on the highly polished desk.

I was sitting about two feet from her desk, at my highly polished desk. I was on the phone to Pall Mall doing my daily task of recording bank figures, to be given later to AEB, Arthur Edward Bryant. My boss, her father.

'Hi Ian, how are you?'

ZZZZZZZ

'Fine, and you, Ann?'

'Very well . . .Thank you.'

More loud snoring coming from Angela. I was finding it difficult to hear Ian. Then I thought he was going to say 'and here are the scores from the United Kingdom . . . Ireland eight points. *Irlande huit points*.' But, no, he gave me the figures and I recorded them and hung up the phone.

In the coolness of this long dark office, which smelt of Neutradol air freshener and Mr Sheen to mask the stench of smoke and booze, there was always a fresh bouquet of flowers in the corner of the room, usually lilies, on a glass table. The office was always quiet and calm. It reminded me of a funeral parlour. I sighed and wondered how did I get here.

Well, I took this secretarial position when I was offered it by Angela, three months earlier. The money was good and the job seemed straightforward enough. There I was, in a little black skirt and jacket with a white collar attached to it. My mother bought it for me in A-Wear. It did look the part. I looked the part. Angela interviewed me and offered the job on the spot. I was delighted and couldn't wait to tell my parents that I'd got a great job in London, after nearly four months looking.

My first day, I left early. It would take about an hour to get there. Metropolitan line into Baker Street, then take the Bakerloo line to Embankment, then the Central line, just two stops to Mansion House tube station. A short walk down Bow Lane, which was really nice, loads of coffee shops and wine bars. Plenty of smart city folk walking fast with briefcases and suits. All very important. Huh, somebody told me once that all they have in their briefcases is a sandwich and a hairbrush. And me there as good as the rest of them, walking swiftly to the rhythm of the city. At the other end of Bow Lane was Cheapside, a large, wide street full of high-street shops. Nearby was St Paul's Cathedral, where I often sat outside on the steps and ate a Boots sandwich and thought if my parents could see me now.

That was before I knew Angela was a raving alcoholic and was having an affair with some bloke called Nigel.

I called her The Woman who Walked into Doors on account of the bruises she'd get when she was well on it. She could easily get through two, maybe even three, bottles in a day. She would order two cases of Petit Chablis for the monthly board meetings and by the time the meetings were on the wine would be gone, so she would send me out discreetly to buy two bottles from the local wine merchants. Francoise and me were on first name terms. But Angela was nice to me and I was loyal to her. One morning she came in with a brown paper bag covering a six-pack of Heineken Export. She said she was being naughty for breakfast.

EDEL BURKE

Passages

I had spent the day with my friend Karyn in London. She was older, already had her twenty-first. We were in a class of student psychiatric nurses, nine of us, seven fellas and Karyn and myself. In a way, we were ready-made friends, paired together like ballroom dancers. I was just eighteen when we started, so to me she had it all.

On arrival, Karyn had rebranded herself from Karen, said it was more sophisticated, more like the English. She was spidery thin, taller than me by a few inches. I couldn't get over the confidence of someone who'd change the spelling of their name. Her favourite jeans were her skin-tight stretch denim that she frequently wore wet because there wasn't enough time to wash and dry them before she'd need to wear them again. She loved to parade herself in them. So while I was at the pool table, she happily went up and down to the bar for whoever needed drinks.

We were on our way back to the hospital having spent the day shopping. We had begun our stint of training on night duty so had to get back. Delayed by my indecisiveness, we hoped to catch the early evening train. It was a half-hour journey to south Hertfordshire where the hospital was. Overwhelmed by the grandeur of St. Pancras station and confined within the barrel shape of the curved roof, we had to move at pace. The assuredness of the wrought iron girders against the fragility of the glass panels left us feeling dwarfed and timid as we ducked right and left of commuters.

We jumped on a train at the first chance and made our way to a smoking carriage. And as if they had followed suit, they announced their arrival, at least ten of them.

'One nil.' Clap clap clap.

'One nil.' Clap clap clap.

They threw their bomber jackets on empty seats and continued to stand the length of the aisle as they raised their arms and chant to barbarous proportions.

'One nil.' Clap clap clap.

'One nil.' Clap clap clap.

Clap, clap, clap, clap.

Clap, clap.

Everyone else was silenced by the uniformity of the chant, the tone, the volume, their appearance. They lined up like overgrown schoolboys dressed in straight denim jeans, Union Jack t-shirts with cut-off sleeves and braces. All topped with grade two haircuts that left a thin film of bristle as coarse as their overused voices.

Shortly after the train pulled out they took their seats, their feet laced high in Doc Martens boots planted firmly on the table beside pint bottles of cider.

Between chants they spat or threw bottle caps. I had the misfortune to light a cigarette and before I had it out of my mouth I heard, 'Who wants a cigarette then?' He took the pack and offered them round. 'She doesn't mind, do you?'

I was afraid to answer for every reason as well as my accent. So I smiled and nodded in agreement, although in my mind it was much more of a kow-tow. The Indian man opposite whispered to just ignore them but I kept my face braced in a smile, hoping that if they liked me they wouldn't harm me. The more cider they drank the more frequent the chanting became but it was no longer just football scores. Even the vowel sounds changed and the tone of their chanting reached a lower depth. Uttered with the accomplishment of a practised choir, every chant started and ended with an 'Ooh, ooh, ooh.'

Its menace pulsated through every vestibule of the train. At each stop the carriage emptied another bit. Then the Indian man got up to leave. They stood three deep to prevent him and threatened to pour the piss from the bottle that one of them had used a couple of minutes earlier. He bowed just like me and, with a bit of jostling and elbowing and a last slap across the back of the neck for good measure, they let him through with a sprinkling of piss, like he was being blessed with holy water. We had hoped to maybe slip out after him, move further down the train but again the chanting and sense of victory seemed to have a swelling effect so we sat tight.

I had never witnessed anything like them and felt shunted between the fascination of wanting to look, to examine every detail, and the visceral terror of wanting to flee. My body was caught in the rhythm of its pulse, my mind terrified of its impulse. I had never seen Karyn so subdued. In the time I had been living there I had become proficient in a lot of things. Karyn had guided me through most of them but even she had no discursive for this one, no ditch lights to gauge the formation.

But I was able to teach Karyn things too. The one lesson she was always grateful for was when I corrected her on her pronunciation of the word 'teeth'. I had become much more attuned to how things sounded and, being an elocution graduate, I waited until I simply couldn't hold back any longer. Her last gesture before we'd go out at night would always be to flash her teeth and ask, 'Are my *theeth* clean?' And I would say yes, except this time I said, 'You mean teeth.'

'Yeah, that's what I said.'

'No, you didn't, you said *theeth*.'

'Say it again.'

'Teeth.'

'No, the two of them together.'

'Teeth, *theeth*.'

'Which one is right?

'Teeth.'

'What do I say?'

'*Theeth.*'

'Oh Jesus Christ, why didn't you stop me before now? So what is it?'

'Teeth.'

'*Theeth*, is that right'?

'No, teeth.'

'*Theeth*. Shit, show me.'

'Don't put your tongue against your teeth so soon, wait until the end of the word.'

'*Theeth.*'

'Ta-eeth.'

'Teeth.'

'You've got it.'

'Thank God. Imagine, I could have lived my life not knowing.' And that, in Karyn's world, would have been *pure disaster*.

*

We didn't often fall out but occasionally there were tensions. Like the time I was selected to represent the school at a local Rotary event. They were having an international summer party. I was kind of put out by the invite, it wasn't the kind of thing I'd want to do on my own. Karyn on the other hand was really put out that I was selected and not her.

'How could he just pick you on your own, sure I'd be much better at that. Are you sure he didn't say the two of us?'

But he hadn't, so that Sunday, I listened to Carole King all morning. I had bought *Tapestry* the previous pay day and couldn't stop playing it over and over. Swathed in thoughts of hope and love and insulated in the comforts of friendship, I walked the two miles to town. I passed gardens full of peony roses that reminded me of my grandmother's but I didn't feel lonely like I normally would.

I was good at smiling and being polite so I hoped once more that would get me through. I was less good at small talk and still way too self-conscious about the sound of my accent. The afternoon passed in a glut of greetings and handshakes. I met fellow internationals and at times actually felt a bit inadequate at being only *Irish*.

'Ah yes, the *Irish*, I'm a sucker for the *Irish*.'

I hadn't a clue as to how I might respond to that, so I just smiled. It felt strange being defined in that way although I knew the intent was good. I suppose I felt a bit smaller on the balance of things.

But then I was approached by someone my own age. He said he had come with his Dad and had spent the afternoon trying to avoid him. So I suppose I was a sort of stop-gap, except we got on; it turned out we had lots in common. We both loved music and soccer, both Chelsea fans. When I told him my cousin had played for Chelsea and that I had held his FA Cup medals in my hand, I think he could have kissed me right there and then, except of course he didn't. We talked guitars, him electric, me acoustic, and how I intended to go to London with my friend Karyn to buy a new one.

And that was where we had been that day on the train, until finally at Borehamwood the football fans got off and the chanting finally stopped. I was never so relieved because at that stage we were only two stops from ours. When our stop came, I saw Simon from the Rotary party get off the next carriage and he came straight over.

'You bought the guitar. I wondered if would you.'

So the guitar was unpacked on the spot and there and then he tried it out for sound, his right foot lifted and resting on a bench.

'A Yamaha, brilliant! Come with us, we're all going to Nigel's, his parents are away. Come on, a party.'

'We can't, we're working tonight.'

'I'll go,' Karyn said, 'we can ring in sick.'

I stood my ground. 'We have to work.'

'I'll go then. Let her off, stick-in-the-mud, that's her.'

She linked Simon and pulled him away. After a few steps he turned, nodded to me to follow but Karyn pulled him closer and with a tug of the arm pulled him round again. I clipped the guitar case shut and walked behind.

I wanted to go with him, not let Karyn take him from me but my sense of responsibility ran deep. By the time we got to the junction, Karyn had made her way back. She said she wouldn't bother with me again if I didn't go, said I needed to grow up, not always do the right thing. So I said OK. But when we got there, it was clear Karyn was determined to get Simon on his own. So I was left sitting with his friends who were drinking shots from bottles in the drinks cabinet. I took a bottle of beer but had no taste for it, so I left. It wasn't that they weren't friendly. I just didn't want to be there.

I walked back to the hospital, dropped the new guitar to the room, changed into my uniform and reported for duty. My apologies for being so late were accepted on the grounds that there was nothing I could do about the train breaking down. I was very quiet in myself that night and for a day or two afterwards. Luckily, the days passed in only sprinkles of light, so I was able to avoid most people, especially Karyn.

But something emerged out of the silence. I had been hoisted like I was lifted up on to my Dad's shoulders, so I could see things better, had an uninterrupted view of how things were. For the first time I saw my own place in things, where I fitted in, how I could manoeuvre my way from one assumption to the other and it didn't matter so much anymore what I sounded like.

Ruth Mac Neely

Becoming Other

She knew she was not a dog. She knew she was not black but she did not know what *Irish* was. Even before she could read she knew those cards on the boards behind glass outside the shops that sold newspapers said something about who she was or wasn't. It always made her mother cross and she would always be reattached tightly to the pram handle, tripping over her sister or sisters as they made their way home, her mother distant and gone.

The mystery of *Irish* took many years to solve. She knew it had to do with this place called *home*. The people around who called to see them or whom they visited on occasion were always talking about *home*. So the house where she lived with her parents was not *home*.

A newspaper, the *Connaught Telegraph*, very different to the daily ones, arrived weekly. The wraparound label addressed in someone's bright blue ink handwriting. the *Connaught Telegraph* was a much-sought-after and passed-around commodity. The refrain, a constant: 'Have you the *Telegraph* and any news from *home*?'

Where they lived was a place called Goldsmith Mansions. From very young she knew this place had something to do with someone called Oliver Goldsmith and he had some connection with *home*. Anything to do with *home* or Ireland was good, she deduced, and anything to do with England was not so good. But she also knew that where she lived was not like where the children who went to her school lived. Around the Mansions most people lived in houses where families had an upstairs and a downstairs with an inside toilet, or else they lived in huge buildings with a lot of floors called flats, which were attractive to her childish eyes. Goldsmith Mansions was dark and infested. Even the open area at the back was just a big patch of earth. No grass, no flowers, not even a wayward bush.

However, she was not allowed down there or even very often out to play. She only ventured into the mystery of the Mansions on very rare occasions, going to the stairs that were barely there, up to visit the Timlins or the Murtaghs. Beneath the stairs was the scariest place of all time. A black hole. No lights on the landings or corridors. Much heard but unseen, scurrying underfoot. *Landlord* was a word she heard early, as was the word *Rachman*. Gradually, she deduced that she was *other*. In small, slow ways that left her puzzled more than anything else. Outside of school, she rarely heard an accent other than an Irish and usually a Mayo one. Her sense of difference eventually added up.

Very close to the Mansions was a place called Peckham Settlement which was a place she and her sister were allowed to go to on a Saturday morning and on some days during the week. The children from the flats used to go there fairly regularly. It was a charity set up to help the poor in the area and at the time it was for her a benevolent place with games, toys, other children and kind, soft-spoken adults, not like the ones she knew. The adults in her life were raucous somehow, loud and laughing when they were together. The people who visited her house and who pulled pennies out from behind her ears or pretended they were slicing their thumbs or who tickled her tummy unmercifully, loudly laughing at her discomfort, often had a sweet, strange smell on their breath. There was always an edge to them which kept her alert.

In the settlement there was a kind lady called Penny who spoke differently but who took an interest in her and her sister. One day news filtered out that a princess was coming to visit the Settlement. The prospect and anticipation of seeing a real princess was almost uncontainable. Though in reality she did not know what a princess was, she had heard a few fairy tales and she knew everyone was pure excited. It was Princess Margaret. She had heard the name for sure. The children from the Settlement were going to be presented to the princess and two of the children who lived in the Mansions were going to present her with a gift. There was talk of little else for some days.

Around the same time, just after beginning school, she started to learn Irish dancing at the Agnes O'Connell School of Irish Dancing. In hindsight she could not say whether she liked it or not. But she ached with all her heart for the black patent leather shoes with huge silver buckles that made that banging noise when you danced. She longed for a pair of those.

In the days before the princess's visit she noticed loud and cross talk from the front room where her parents slept. The door of the bedroom was left slightly ajar in the early evening so that her parents could hear the baby in the cot at the foot of the bed. She knew her mother was happy for her to meet the princess but the loud, cross words that were nightly repeated at the time were words like *them* and *us* and *English* and maybe even *Catholic*.

Eventually she was told that the event clashed with an Irish dancing concert and she was not allowed to go. She had no idea what it all meant. Her princess excitement had been short-lived and her heart bore the brunt of a disappointment she could not understand. The Timlin twins were presenting Princess Margaret with flowers. How could she not be there? Why could she not go to see a princess? Why couldn't the Irish dancing wait? She vaguely remembers being on the stage, dancing. She never graduated beyond slippers and never got the black shiny shoes with the silver buckle. It was the first of many, many puzzles on the way to becoming *Irish*.

Walking back from shops not far from the Mansions one Sunday with a younger child in tow, the Sunday streets were almost silent. She was probably sent out earlier for either a rare treat of sweets or else a packet of fags. The nearer shops were closed, so she was on an unusual foray to more distant shops. This meant that there was some sort of gathering on at *home* because she would not normally be allowed out. Her parents must have been preoccupied. Visitors, most likely.

On her way back, down the narrow and dark Staffordshire Street, which had few houses, she had reached the high windowless wall of the pickle factory and was nearly at the corner turn for the Mansions when she was set upon by a group of children. No adult was around and the street was empty. These children all went to the Protestant school that she had to pass everyday to get to her own school, St Francis's. Among them were twin girls she knew by sight, the leaders of this little gang. She cowered against the wall of the factory, holding on tight to the little one but not knowing what she was going to do. She was no more than six or seven. There is little memory of what was said only the tension of difference and name and the imminence of some kind of beating. But then she heard someone roar 'Scat, leave them alone!' in a familiar voice that brought waves of relief over her tense little body.

It was that most beloved person, Uncle Johnnie, the uncle who was 'no good for anything', the one who drank too much and could not hold down a job but whose kindness to her and her sisters meant smuggled comics, smuggled sweets and, on one wonderful occasion, 'real' toy telephones that came for Christmas but had to be returned the day after because they weren't paid for. But that was Johnnie. The joy was short-lived always because the comics or the sweets or the toys or the coins would be discovered and there would be hell to pay. Too-loud words, cowering children and Johnnie pinned against the wall by her father, one balled fist in his chest and an elbow under his chin. He never retaliated. Always, he would catch her eye and smile a little. He never seemed afraid. Many years later she realised this was not so.

And then there was that time the baby went down the hole in the ground and disappeared forever. Her baby brother who stopped her mother noticing her, her baby brother who took away even the occasional soft touch, even when she had a toothache. All softness left, all ease, not that there had ever been too much. She had become a nuisance. She remembers ever after longing for a soft touch from her mother. There was none after he disappeared. She remembered his little white coffin leaving the front room of the Mansions, her mother on the floor, beside herself, the dark winter day, her father cold with rage. Her baby brother disappeared down the hole in the ground and was lost forever. Her parents buried him in a strange graveyard in South London, Brenchley Gardens. The snow falling on his little coffin on a cold February day. There were no visitors from *home*.

They were undone completely.

When she was nearing her mid-forties, in a loose conversation, she found out that whilst the funeral was detailed in her childish mind, she had in fact been in Ireland. She had always believed she was there when his coffin left the dark front room but she was being minded by strangers called *grandparents* and *relations*.

She was undone completely.

Across the River with my Father

On occasional Sundays
   And I mean occasional
   We visited
   The Tower of London
   Buckingham Palace
   Downing Street
   The Houses of Parliament
   Trafalgar Square
   The National Art Gallery
   The Cenotaph
   Westminster Abbey and Cathedral.
   Big Ben, museums, parks, churches.

All manner of histories unravelled.
   The lump-in-the-throat Tomb
   of the Unknown Soldier.
   Unknowing, not known to me then.
   A line of bishops, princes, kings, queens,
   Children kept in towers, marriages,
   Beheadings, wars, six-fingered wives,
   Several Thomases – à Becket, Cromwell, More.
   Martyrs.

Crossing the Thames on a big red bus.
   Dressed in a dress tied at the back with a bow.
   White socks, neat hair, ribbons, clips and ponytails.
   Perhaps, but only perhaps, an ice cream cone.
   Crossing the river, crossing the Thames.

Initiated
   Into the great Irish confusion,
   Into your great Irish confusion.

Bernadette Davies-McGreal

Homecoming How Ar' Ya!

The sun was streaming in through the big-paned window of our eleventh-floor flat in leafy north-west London, one of the many tower blocks to be built in the 1960s. The walls could lay testament to the fact that many a day we would have Ray Lynam, Philomena Begley and Big Tom, to name but a few, blasting out of those windows. 'Run to the Door' was like a Sunday missal in our home. Why Big Tom had to run to the door I will never know. We lived half way up the twenty-two storey block; in fact, you could call our family the 'in-betweeners'. Mum and Dad being a combination of Welsh and Irish contributed to the fact that wherever we went we were 'blow-ins', regarded neither as English in England, nor Irish in Ireland, nor Welsh in Wales. It didn't help that our block of flats fell between Fellows Road and Adelaide Road, which meant that our address could be one or the other, just like our nationality.

My Dad and I had just got in off the number thirty-one bus after a Saturday visit to Camden Town. Having waited nearly forty-five minutes for the bus, we now climbed the endless steps at the front of the block and then waited another ten minutes for the lift. We were exhausted. The fact that Dad had insisted on having a drink on the way back at the Man in the Moon in Chalk Farm didn't help. Of course it would never be just the one. He'd have a couple of his favourite Czech lagers, always keen to try something new since he discovered Mr Wetherspoon, followed by a Hennessy brandy to finish up. He loved the brandy so much that they had even named the dog after it back home.

Sitting there in the pub, he looked more Irish than Ireland itself, his hat placed elegantly on the polished veneer table and his stick alongside his leg, acting as a prop. He always looked so dapper and had a big smiley red face to polish it off. Coming out, we would often be delayed by Dad introducing me to newfound friends, mainly Irish, but sometimes the odd 'foreigner' too. He often told me he learnt more about Irish history from an Argentinian tourist in London than he ever did at Murrisk School, back in the day. It was more about collecting sticks for the classroom fire and bringing in the odd sod of turf for the master back then.

'Put the kettle on, there's a good girl.' No matter how old I was getting I was still a 'good girl'.

'OK, do you want anything with the tea?'

Dad had always been a relatively quiet man and of impeccable appearance. He was always in the shirt and tie, whether at work or play, and today was no different. He had a stick but spent more time doing an impersonation of Charlie

Chaplin than anything else. Proud, dead proud, that seemed to be the motto of the McGreal family. Admitting they needed help would be something of a challenge. I would say this had been deeply instilled in him as a child and he never shelved this pride in where he came from.

'Some soda bread. I got it in Marks, it's in the cupboard. It's a meal in itself. I cooked some Corrigan sausages, they're in the fridge. Ah you canna beat the taste.'

Dad came from the Deerpark, a place of true beauty overlooking Clew Bay in the shadow of Croagh Patrick. He never lost his accent; it was still as strong as the day he stepped off the boat at Holyhead in 1947, 'the year of the big snow'. He would often begin his reply with this when anyone cared to ask how long ago he had left the auld sod. Landing in Blighty, he got a job initially working for Wimpey Construction. He never imagined when he left P.J. Kelly's that he would be about to spend the next eighteen months in the Yemen. Yes, the Yemen. 'Jesus, Mary and Joseph, the heat was unbearable, man,' as he so often reminded us. We never got to know much about it but would see the odd photo of him posing on a bulldozer in the middle of the desert. I wish I could ask him now but the memory is not much cop, as he would say.

Dad picked up his black holdall and put it onto the G-Plan table. It was the holdall he used for his day-to-day shopping and also his flights back and forth to Knock. Dual purpose you could say, like his nationality. The bag had seen better days; it had been stolen from him once as he sat in the Ice Wharf in Camden Lock. The punters had felt so sorry for him that they took to the streets looking for the culprit. Unbeknown to them it only contained his favourite Cumberland pie from Marks and was found a couple of streets away, pie and bag intact.

He took out three bars of Cussons Imperial Leather soap and the Wilkinson Sword blades and placed them carefully upon the table. Now we were home, I felt I ought to say something.

'Er, Dad, you know the soap?' I was hesitant, not wanting to upset him in what had now become a ritual.

'What about it?'

I passed Dad the tea, Sainsbury's Red Label, the closest he could get to Irish tea, he claimed. The soap and blades were for his brothers, you see.

'Well, the thing is the last time I was over I saw plenty of soap in Westport and I don't think they will let me on the plane with the blades. The O'Leary man has got ever so strict you know,' I said in a timid fashion.

'What are you talking about?'

'They can buy soap and blades in Westport now, Dad. There is no need for you to worry about sending them over anymore.'

The brothers used to laugh at him when he landed home and put the soap and blades on the table, a leg-pulling part of the ritual expected at any homecoming, though less so when their parents were alive. Or maybe I was just too young to realise what was going on.

Dad looked a little perplexed and his face took on a rather bemused expression. I hated this; I knew he would be upset; this was just one of his contributions to back home, albeit small. It was always in his mindset. Niggling away in his conscience. He was always looking after them, putting things by for them all the time, saving newspaper cuttings. 'BIGGEST PIG EVER DIES, 900 KILOS.' Anything animal-related got cut out: stories about cows, horses, sheep. You name it, he saved them and posted them back to the Deerpark.

'Dad?' I called out. I didn't want to hurt his feelings. How could I ever know the reasoning behind his longing to help them?

'Ah sure, you take them anyway,' he said in a resigned fashion.

What will I do with them, I thought to myself. I suppose I should be grateful that he wasn't like his brother Pat, who insisted on taking up two seats on the bus to Holyhead, with his work tools and bricks. Yes, bricks. I never worked out if he was worried they'd get nicked while he was away from his bedsit in Holloway for two weeks or if his tools were that much better than what awaited him on his return to the farm. It beggars belief how he got the eagle statue over, which sits proudly in front of the homestead to this day. This is the same uncle who shared digs with Dad when he first came over to London and who caught a rabbit at one of the building sites, thinking it would make a great pet for us in the tower block. Needless to say, we brought it to a pet shop in Parkway after only a couple of days.

He changed the subject hesitantly. 'I washed a few shirts there.'

'OK Dad, I will put the iron over them in a little while.' I felt bad. I should have just taken the soap and blades without saying anything. It was as if all these little things he did in some way eased things for them back home.

'Ah they're alright. Don't be worrying. Rest yourself. You won't be going for a while, will ya? Oh and there's, ah, some old shirts of mine there to take back to the boys. They'll be fine for up the land.'

Dad got up and went into the kitchen. He turned on the radio. In front of him was a Wetherspoon menu of drinks, with 'PETER' in big letters written across the top, no doubt ready to be put with the soap and blades, to be sent over for his brothers' benefit. I felt he was never alone when he had his radio beside him. At the flick of a switch, he could be back with the showbands in Ireland and down memory lane once more.

Dad would always claim that England had been good to him. He was only ever told to go back to his own country once, by a reputable actor in Hampstead outside a scouts' club in the 1970s. Ronald Fraser was his name. It is ironic, to say the least, that Fraser appeared in a TV series called *The Misfit*, playing a character who was supposedly loyal, faithful and loved people whatever their colour or creed. Suffice to say Dad could not confirm this from his personal experience of him that night. We used to always grin when he came on the telly, remembering this incident and teasing Dad about it. He would try to hold back his laughter but would join in eventually. I guess it reminded him of the time when he arrived in the big city and the signs on the windows of the lodgings. Strange, that when he did eventually return, the welcome was not altogether what you would have expected from his own.

It wasn't long before Dad joined me back in the front room. The sun was shining on the picture in the centre of the wall, reflecting on the glass frame of an oil painting which was always a topic of conversation. As a surprise, Mum had arranged for a Welsh artist to paint a picture of Dad's home place, modelled on a John Hinde postcard. You were never too far from the Deerpark, you see, even in the centre of London, with all its hustle and bustle. The walls were decorated in large-patterned red floral wallpaper which had been up since the 1960s and this gave the painting the dramatic backdrop it so richly deserved. The painting took pride of place on the eleventh floor, overlooking the whole of London. The view from the flat was not dissimilar to being on the top of Croagh Patrick, in fact. Instead of mountains and islands, it was a landscape of roofs, smoke and landmarks like Hampstead Heath, the Brecknock Arms, Holloway, Camden, Highgate, Chalk Farm, Kentish Town. It was like a three-dimensional A to Z.

After sitting in the chair for a short while, Dad got up and went to the dresser. It was still adorned with mementoes from each of the homelands. Two large white dogs sat presumptuously beside the two proud golden horses, purchased in the 1970s from O'Grady's in The Mall. Statues of the Child of Prague, with its badly glued head, and St Patrick were looking down on them from the second shelf, along with a shillelagh and the decanter set that had been sent all the way from America after his sister was killed. Dad was always a keen shopper and when he went to Ireland alone he would invariably return with Irish-themed presents for us and linen tea cloths for Mum, with instructions on how to make an Irish stew or Irish coffee. There was always the need to bring a little bit of Ireland home with him, in whatever shape or form. But his clothes hid the best present of all, the smell of the turf fire.

We as a family could profess to be fluent in all Irish sayings and recipes at this stage. In later years, Dad's bag would be filled with biscuits – Kimberleys, Mikados, Coconut Creams – and chocolates. Dad's friend John Murphy on the fourth floor would always put in an order for Carrageen moss and dillisk from his bar stool in The Washington.

I was away with the fairies, as they say, because I did not notice Dad holding out his hand to me, saying, 'Here, take it.'

'Sorry Dad, I was just thinking.'

'Here's two hundred for now, get something nice in Westport.'

'Ah Dad. Thank you. You know you don't have to.'

'The weather should be good this time of year, there's some nice shops opened up down the quay, get yourself a scarf or something, and buy Peter and Frank a drink in Campbell's, and tell them I was asking after them, and tell Owen I said hello.'

'Ah Dad. Thanks.'

'I used to run there, you know, at the Point. I did surely.'

I glanced over at the dresser and there were his medals taking pride of place beside his attendance certificate as a volunteer with the Irish navy. I recollected him saying he had trained in Galway for ten shillings a week. Alongside these sat his medals for safe driving. He had driven for over twenty years, delivering cigarettes out of a Crouch End depot and never smoking one himself. The continuous dream of returning to Ireland was never very far from his mind while driving his Bedford van across the length and breadth of London.

In fact, it was only a matter of a few years until his dream became a reality, when we both decided to leave the smoke and return to live in Ireland. Yet in the year of 'The Gathering', which was supposed to welcome home all emigrants, I saw him staring at a padlocked gate leading to his beloved home. The dancer Jean Butler even featured his homestead in her 'love letter' to Ireland, encouraging emigrants to return home. Yet here was Dad, not able to get into his. You see, with an ailing uncle and the flick of a pen, the one thing that had kept the family together for decades was lost to an abyss of memories. The link in the chain had been replaced by a padlock.

Homecoming how ar' ya!

SUSAN GRAHAM

Legacy

There has been a further delay on Aer Lingus flight EI911 to Ireland West Knock.

'What can you do, like?'

She glanced up at him over her magazine. These were the first words spoken between them in the half hour they had been sitting across from each other in the lounge in Gatwick. She had, however, been covertly observing him, a habit formed over years of travelling alone. The habit entertained her, firing up her imagination as she wove stories around tired, lined faces or garbled words or shabby clothes. He met none of the above criteria; in fact it was his eyes that initially caught her attention. They were attention-seeking, no doubt about it. Large, blue-grey, edged with the longest, darkest lashes she had ever seen on a man and an expression in them she had been attempting to put into words that didn't sound clichéd. Longing? Lost? Childlike? But there was something sharp too, a bitterness that was almost pungent and if you focused on that bitterness, then it was hard to see the other, softer side. Overall, the effect was quite scary and yet somehow captivating at the same time. They were eyes you would either fall for or run from and she had both fallen and run quite enough in her lifetime. So she sat solidly, wanting to know more about him, but happy that the time was limited by the vagaries of the Atlantic wind howling over Knock Airport. Although they were obviously on the same flight, she knew she would be met and scooped away by her daughter immediately on landing, so there was no fear of prolonging the connection.

'It's always the same this time of year. Just as long as we don't get diverted to Shannon.'

He tipped his pint to her in acknowledgement of the wish. He had been supping steadily since she sat down and this was his third that she knew of, but there was no apparent intoxication. His clothes were decent, casual, but his shoes were highly polished, which she always thought said a lot about a man. Hungry, that was the word that best suited his eyes. Not a sexual hunger, but there was a definite craving there, maybe for recognition, or nurture. She needed to find out, so in she plunged.

'Are you going home?'

'Going home?'

His tone voiced the bitterness she saw in his eyes. The accent was unalloyed Cockney. She knew it well because her mother had been born in the East End, within the reverberating clang of Bow Bells. She also knew from her personal history that accent meant little or nothing when it came to Ireland potentially being that place you called home.

'Sorry,' he said. 'This airport is probably the closest thing to home. More like a half-way house. I don't belong here and I don't belong there, not with my accent. "Are you enjoying your visit to Mayo? Is it your first time here? Where are you staying?" It drives me mad, when I've probably spent half my life there. I don't even bother to explain any more that I stayed every summer and Christmas, from the age of three, half way up a mountain in Ballycastle, til I got to an age where they couldn't drag me over any more, especially not at Christmas. It just wasn't Christmassy enough in Mayo. Not enough lights, not enough action, too much religion.'

'I know what it's like,' she said. 'The times I have been told that I have to wait for my Guinness to settle. I regularly say "I've been drinking it from before you were born" but sometimes I'm too weary to bother.'

'What's your story then?'

'English born,' she replied. 'Still have a touch of the old accent. Lived in Ireland from the age of fourteen, never worked anywhere else. Just been over to my auntie's funeral in London. You?'

'Born in London, me old dear's from Mayo, Dad from Garryspillane down in Limerick, famous for hurlers. Mind you, she says the only hurling he did was late at night into the gutter after drinking too much. They met in the Shamrock Club in the Elephant and Castle in '67. She was a good bit older than him, worked in a sausage factory and was out for a good time, which they had and which was how I came to be. Problem was, he had another girlfriend in London and got her pregnant too and chose her to do the decent thing with, going back to Limerick to get married.'

'She kept you though, your mother, if you visited Mayo as a child. That must have been hard back in those days.'

'Yeh,' he nodded. 'I'd say it was. That was why I was three the first time I went on the ferry to Ireland. Granny was religious and if it was down to her, I might never have been accepted into the family, but Grandad was a very kind man and must have got round her. When the day came for us to head back to England, Grandad and my mum would spend the whole morning crying. It was a bloody nightmare. I wasn't used to all that emotion. I'd never seen my mum crying, only at those times.'

'What was it like growing up without a dad, or did she marry someone else?'

'No, she never married. She lives in a nursing home now in Castlebar, never had any more kids. Worked all her life in dead-end jobs to keep us fed and pay the rent on the flat off the Walworth Road. But I always felt I was better off without a dad. All the dads on my estate were either missing or bloody layabouts who would beat up the missus and kids when they came home drunk after spending the children's allowance and pissing it up against a wall. It was the women who kept a roof over everyone's head and kept them fed, whether they took a beating or not. So I considered myself lucky.'

The bitterness went from his eyes and they welled up as he talked.

'School was all women too. The dinner ladies were Irish. I reckon every school dinner lady in London was Irish back then. They gave us massive dinners. Most of the kids were from Irish families with a scattering of Jamaicans. O'Neill, McNamara, Lynch and Wilson. All my mates from the flats started in St Joseph's Primary together and went on up to the Sacred Heart Secondary together. Back to school in September after the summer holidays was a joke. "What I did in my summer holidays." Every one of us wrote, "Went to Ireland. Helped out on the farm, tramping cocks of hay, bringing the turf home." That was the holidays every year. I don't know why the teacher bothered. Our mums thought we were all little angels. There was no discipline or structure. They got us anything we wanted. The winos in the park would play soccer with us when they sobered up a bit. Then the likes of Hairy Paddy would go back to his bottle of meths and start swigging and crying "I'll never go home again". On their arses and still reminiscing about Ireland. The ones in London were always on about going home to Ireland and the ones gone back to Ireland kept on about London and how good it had been and what they missed. Never fucking happy anywhere. Sorry for the language.'

He was starting to slur a bit and was getting worked up. She considered making her excuses, bathroom or something, but curiosity got the better of her.

'Would you eat this sandwich? I've had enough with the one half. I'm getting another cup of tea. Will I get you one?'

'No tea thanks, I'll stick with the beer but I'll take you up on that sandwich if you're sure you don't want it.'

'I'm sure. Go ahead. Be back in a minute.'

He was calmer by the time she returned with the tea.

'So did you stay living in London?'

'I tore the arse out of it in London. Like I was saying, the mums treated us like princes. We were the men in their lives and we could do no wrong. Irish mums, you've got to love 'em. No discipline or structure, come and go as you like, no questions asked. At fifteen, sixteen, we were walking time bombs and surrounded by drink and drugs. We'd be out on the razzle constantly. We had our own way of laying our hands on dough. In and out of work. I was a postman for a while, thought it would be a handy number. But it was all stairs, dogshit and people looking for their dole cheques. In the end I used to post everything back into the postbox because I couldn't be arsed climbing any more stairs. Got my marching orders of course. There's a good few blanks around those years. In the end, I knew I had to get out or I'd be dead before much longer. Moved to Dublin where I knew no-one.'

Passengers for flight EI911 to Ireland West Knock please go to Gate 15 for immediate boarding.

'That's us. Cheers for the sandwich.'

She couldn't let him get away without her finding out more, so she moved quickly to be close to him in the queue at the check-in desk. The flight wasn't full and she managed to find an empty spot beside him, although he did give her a look as she sat down in the aisle seat.

'I'm not stalking you. I would just love to hear how life has worked out for you, that is, if you don't mind.'

'It doesn't end well, if that's what you're looking for.'

'No I'm not . . . that is . . . whatever. Sorry, you must think I'm really nosey.'

'For a woman not born Irish you've certainly picked up their ways, asking too many bloody questions. I'm going to Killala. I'm hoping to see my kids. She couldn't put up with my drinking any more. Being pissed has become part of me. My old man died in Limerick at forty-eight, the booze killed him. I never learnt how to be a proper father or husband. I'll never be a Paddy and wouldn't be accepted as one anyway. Not with this accent. I don't know where I belong. My mum does nothing but complain when I visit her. She wants to be in the family home up the mountains but it's falling down and rotten with damp. I just give up.'

He closed his eyes. Those gorgeous eyelashes were wet again. She sat quietly for a while, struggling with her conscience. There was nothing she could say after all that, so stretching out her arm she rested her hand lightly on him, leaving it there as he slept all the way to Ireland West Knock.

SÉAMUS MCNALLY

Ebb and Flow

Tony placed his bet on number five, running in the 2.30 at Sandown Park. He then crossed the busy Wembley Road and went back into Mannion's public house. He moved through the Saturday regulars, mainly Irish, to where Yorkie was still sitting next to Tony's pint with a silly grin.

'So, you have placed your last bet on English soil, Tony O'Toole? Ladbrokes will call in the receiver after the loss of their biggest loser.'

'No loss to me; betting's a mug's game. One thing I won't miss going back home is the bookies.'

'You'll be too busy with the big ranch.'

'Well, I know who to ring if I need a cowboy. Come on, fire that piss into you and we'll get the van loaded.'

'I hope you've got gloves. I don't want my fingerprints all over them tools if you get stopped at customs.'

'Now, now Yorkie, everything going into that van is legit, earned with my own sweat and blood.'

'With a little sponsorship from Wimpey and John Lang.'

'Them boys won't miss the odd Kango or stray wheelbarrow.'

This was typical of the banter for a month now, ever since Tony announced he was going back home. Yorkie knew the score. Tony had inherited the farm at home twenty years previously. Although his younger brother lived there and worked the farm, his father had signed over the place to Tony. The tradition was to give the place to the eldest, though most people didn't hold to that any longer. But the auld fella had married late and was set in an older way of thinking.

Tony could have signed the place over to the young brother but it made no sense, giving away your inheritance. Might even bring bad luck. He always saw the brother as a temporary caretaker. Sow a bit of wild oats in England before ploughing a new furrow at home. Meanwhile, P.J. was content at home minding Mother.

Tony was thinking his thoughts and Yorkie studied the form in *The Sun* as they drove the red Transit in silence. Now was the time. He had informed the brother of his intention in a phone call at Christmas. He could tell it shook them up a bit, both P.J. and Mother. Still, they all knew he intended to return at some stage. Hadn't he steered clear of any close relationships in England, just so as not to risk complications when he decided to move back?

England had changed. Most of the Irish had moved back to the good times at home. But he wasn't ready then.

'What will P.J. do?' Yorkie asked.

Tony didn't care what P.J. did. It was his decision to stay at home and mind

Mother. And anyway, why had she married a man twenty years her senior, a man who had already left her a widow for the past eighteen years?

'You'll never settle back now,' Yorkie continued. Earlier he had bought Tony a cheap map of Ireland in the Pakistani shop across from the station. Yorkie thought that was hilarious. 'Here,' he says. 'You'll need this to find your way home after going missing for twenty years.'

'I know exactly where I'm going so you can stick your map. And don't bother keeping it to plan a visit back because I won't be inviting you.'

But Yorkie, the big, thick Leitrim man who had earned his nickname from Tony because of his favourite chocolate bar, wouldn't stop, insisted on giving Tony 3/1 that he would be back within a year. The fifty pound bet was safe with Christy behind the counter.

They drove down the back lane behind the houses, which gave access to the garage. Tony had bought the house a decade earlier at a good price. He had divided it into flats for rent and kept one for himself. The garage at the back was handy for storing the tools he sometimes took from the many sites he worked on. He had built up a nice cache of equipment that would come in useful at home.

'You going to give P.J. your flat here?' Yorkie asked, looking up at the house.

'If that's what he wants and he pays the going rate,' replied Tony. 'He would be a handy caretaker but I've done the sums. It would be cheaper to use a letting agency and rent the flat.' That was Tony's reasoning. 'Anyways, haven't I given him twenty-five years of free rent at home. Time he started to pay his way.'

P.J. placed his black Raleigh bicycle against the gable of Sarah Carey's house. He had seen her baking bread at the kitchen table and now she was at the back door before him, shaking flour from her hands.

'Hello, P.J. Just baking some brown bread,' was her greeting.

'Has to be done. I baked one for Mother this morning,' replied P.J.

'How is she keeping?'

'Not bad, good. That's why I came down. I want to go out with Mother on Tuesday and I thought you might get her ready.'

'Oh, that's nice, going out together, I mean.'

'It's what she'd like. Not being left behind on her own.'

'So, what time will I go down?'

'Come down at eleven. That way she'll be ready for the Angelus at midday. She wouldn't want to go out without the Angelus.'

'That's no problem. Will you come in for a cup of tea?'

'No thanks, Sarah. I have things to do, and I haven't started the car for a while.'

'No bother, P.J. Eleven o'clock and I'll have her looking lovely.'

'That's important for her,' he concluded as he rounded the corner of the house.

Tuesday morning had turned sunny by the time P.J. and his mother left the house after midday, waved off by the ever-smiling Sarah Carey. He went around by the long route so that she could see her old family home, and then along the scenic coast road. P.J knew that high tide was at 12.30. Offshore, the big rock, Carrigdoo, was covered already, a sure sign of a spring tide. Mother pointed out familiar landmarks and houses, sometimes including a comment on the people who lived there. Then he took the harbour road rather than drive straight on for the town. Mother didn't mind, on a special day, because she was going out with P.J.

The high tide was almost lapping the top of the harbour wall when P.J. drove into it.

'The car entered the water at 12.40 PM,' the local sergeant recalled at the inquest. Linus O'Leary, the fishing trawler skipper and sole witness, had recorded the time in his log. Sarah Carey had given further evidence of getting Mrs Nora O'Toole ready to go out with her son P.J. on the morning of the tragic drowning. No, she could not recall anything strange in the demeanour of the victims before they set off, just after the Angelus.

The tide still ebbed and flowed in Poldoo as the red Transit van went over Carr's Brae, which always gives the first or last view of the ocean, depending which way you are going. It is the last for Tony O'Toole, hunched over the wheel, unlike his arrival two months earlier, when he cruised gently into view, sunk back in the seat, the better to savour the familiar sights of his childhood. Now there is a ferry to catch.

'Jesus Christ,' he mutters to himself, as if the news of the events had just reached him for the first time. 'Never even got to meet Mother.' Now he knew why P.J. had checked and double-checked the time he expected to arrive. Tony had met Sarah returning to her own place and he had pulled up on the quiet road to greet his childhood neighbour. She had told him how P.J. had just gone out with Mother.

Despite everything that had happened, he still tried to stay. But he knew it was no good. Sure, they had shaken his hand at the funeral because that was the custom, but nobody came near him after that.

'You'll be home within a year,' Yorkie had said. Tony knew he said 'home' deliberately to rile him, but he let it go. Yorkie could have the fifty pounds, still safe, no doubt, behind the bar with Christy. Much safer than Tony felt with the neighbours in Poldoo, after the events. He'd rather settle for the mocking of Yorkie, who he could picture ceremoniously spitting on the fifty-pound note.

Tony wouldn't say anything about the voice, the voice of Aunt Alice, his mother's sister, that had started inside his head a week after the burial. She had long departed this world, but she always was an interfering bitch. He had no idea where she learned the strong language she used on him. Words of abuse and condemnation, to torture him day and night.

Now he is over the brow of Carr's Brae and straightens himself up as he gives the Transit more pedal. Rolling the window down, he shakes his head as if to get his focus back and stirs a couple of ewes on the long acre with his loud shout.

'Well, fuck yourself too, Aunt Alice. I will not do your bidding. I will not take a running jump off anywhere. No! I'm away back home to England, where none of you will have nothing more to say.'

GERALDINE MITCHELL

Gone to Ground

Yet again a clear sky
and the lateral spill of light
over fields, reeds and sea.
Sun laid down like gold leaf.

That day in the woods,
once the party was over,
when they had all gone home,
you had hidden too well,
no-one to find you, only owls
and a badger shuffling.

Break it up,
  let it fall,
pick it up,
  see what shapes
appear.
  Do it again
and again.

Sun laid like gold leaf
over sloping fields,
over the face of each stone,
every tumbled gable end.

You still hidden.
Still unfound.
The boxes in the attic
above the bed.
The suitcase.

I lay your story
on the floor –
you start to hum
you are near.

(Sometimes when we wake
the weight of pain so heavy
we throw the blankets off.)

The suitcase lies tongue-tied as a tomb, secret as thought. On rainy afternoons we dare each other up the cobwebbed stairs, thrill with shapes still blanketed in dark, our own familiar ghosts. A single dusty bulb and out of broken boxes the grope of musty clothes. The ballerina winks an absent eye and then the game can start: my sister susurrates some hocus-pocus prayer and one by one we drop to scabby knees, call up the spirit of our aunt, the one they never talk about, her initials stamped in leather marble-hard.

They came, they went,
who spoke? Who told
the truth? Who stayed
silent as the suitcase?

Who has the voice?
The ones who left?
The ones who stayed?
The ones who died?
The ones still living?

Who listens?

We looked and looked.
Why didn't you cry out?
We stayed after dark.
You didn't move.

PAUL SOYE

As I Remember It

Memories haunt me. Pinpricks, piercing the skin from within, bitter-sweet. The best I could do was to weave them into a narrative, practiced, with its built-in flaws from each re-telling and re-rememberings that have, over time, become myth. That myth has become who I am and I the ghostwriter of my self. Now, looking at the photograph of that youth, in the summer of 1971, with long hair, parka jacket and metallic gold Honda CB 250, it's hard to credit that he ever existed other than in the workshop of the mind. Here I sit, faintly smiling in the glow of something pleasant, reimagining the past – I'm standing beside my Rocinante.

They had me going for a while.

It was dark, past midnight, I stopped under a streetlight, no clue which turn to take – Centre Ville, Paris-Est, Paris L'ouest or Autres Directions. They surrounded me in seconds. Six or eight. I remember thinking, I've had it. They cut their engines, stood their bikes and spoke in French. I was tired and in no mood for messers. Standing one pace clear of the bike, I was determined to give a good account of myself.

They ran their eyes over the 250, touched its curves, saw the tricolour on the mudguard and pointed to me – 'Eer Lawned?' They were all smiles, happy, in admiration, and eager to help. I relaxed, unzipped my parka jacket and showed them the address. My map was hopelessly inadequate, so they indicated that I should follow them.

They led me through the city, long avenues, small side-streets and alleys where the sound of the engines reverberated from the walls of the high buildings. Then through an arch into the courtyard of a palace and, before I could take it in, out through the arch on the far side, along by the river and left. They stopped, pointed to a place name on the side of a building. This was it. Place de la Bastille. They each shook my hand and then, with great noise, disappeared.

Alone; my first night.

The photo was a little faded. Forty-four years old. The building behind me, how I remember it. Nursing home, foyer de retraite. That's the thing with a photograph, it preserves the moment. But the memories, the meaning, that's a different matter. They depend on me, my frame of mind, both then and now; my purpose. I dust them down from time to time and each time they change a little. Just a little. But something of the original lingers, a memory link remains.

As I cast my mind back, I can't say I had any intention of making contact with him, Mrs Delaney's son, when I set out. I told her that I'd try. 'Do,' she said. 'Ray'd be delighted to meet you and help in any way he could.'

Ray was a priest. I reckoned him to be ten or twelve years older than myself. Thirty-one or thirty-two perhaps. He lived with a community of priests on Rue Jacque Coeur just off the Place de la Bastille. Dapper in casual grey, his feet stuck into a pair of broken-backed leather slippers, I stood when he entered the formal parlour in which I had waited. Stiffness liquefied into South Dublinese as we sipped awfully strong coffee. Each evening he walked me around central Paris, off the beaten path, in and out of foyers to see beautiful arches or ornate ceilings; older cafés where philosophers might gather; places where riots had taken place in '68; graffiti ('Je ne dégrade pas. J'écrit'); Shakespeare and Company, old and new, whose owner had published Joyce; the former Hotel d'Alsace, where Wilde spent his last days. Each evening ended with a beer. He spoke softly of essence and existence and patiently listened to a youthful rant on the Church and the oppressive society that spawned us. 'I'm not going back,' I told him. Finally, on the third evening, he called my bluff. He told me he had a friend who might find me a job for the summer, where my lack of French wouldn't be too great a problem. What he read on my face I don't know. 'The offer's there,' he said. 'Sleep on it and call me tomorrow.'

Warm in my sleeping bag in the dark of the campsite near Bois de Vincennes, I reflected on the last three days. Tossed and turned. Before falling asleep, free of everything but myself, I finally made my decision.

I became an emigrant. Happier in my skin. Ray and I met again several times that summer and he confided his 'struggle' with celibacy and spoke about the new hope within the Church – *Humanae Vitae*, liberation theology and the new Catechism. He introduced me to his friend Serge, and without him ever saying anything I understood him to be his lover. I felt no shock, though he watched me carefully as we ate in Serge's apartment, just an acceptance of the essence of it: relationship.

Now, with an address where I could at last receive letters, I began to write home. I wrote about the unfamiliar foods I was tasting. I gave a detailed description of artichoke eating, how you stripped it leaf by leaf until you got to its heart where all the hairy bits needed to be scraped before it was eaten – much ado about nothing, I had written. I described courgettes and aubergines and how it was a bit of a myth that Ireland had the best vegetables in the world. I tried to convey the beauty and wealth of this wonderful city. And I wrote about my new job.

I worked in the *foyer de retraite*. The nursing home was newly built and needed to be fitted, curtains hung, table lamps distributed, and all the furnishings installed before it opened in the autumn. And so it was. The work wasn't very challenging, either physically or mentally. I learnt a good deal of French, most of which would, and did, get me into trouble in polite company, but served me well in my next job. French might not have the equivalent of the one-word Anglo-Saxon profanities with which I was well acquainted, and this led me into a false sense of security. I had, woven into my everyday speech, blasphemies, vulgarities and swear words that sounded innocuous to me, but which were conversation stoppers when I was invited to people's homes.

Before the end of summer and just before the job itself wound up, I headed for Strasbourg, for no other reason than that one of the men at work was from there. He gave me his brother's name, Jean-Marie, and said to look him up.

On the morning of my departure I had coffee with Ray in the parlour in which he had first received me. We said our goodbyes. 'I have something for you,' he said, and he took a book from the top of the sideboard. 'It's one of my own. Keep it and remember that square mile of Paris we visited.' It was *Dubliners*. He came down to the street, waved as I drove away and stood there until I disappeared around the corner.

Jean-Marie was a real find. A character, he became not only my boss but a close friend. He was a little unkempt-looking, which made me wary at first, and he had an unfiltered *Gauloise* cigarette permanently attached to his lower lip. He also had the habit of slurping beer noisily. What he saw in me, a sort of raggle-taggle aimless youth, I don't know. But he was attractively anti-establishment and took the side of the young, troubled teenagers with whom he worked. He guided me through the bureaucratic process of getting a work visa, a French identity card and a room in a shared HLM apartment.

One afternoon I found a note on the table of the apartment. The funding had come through for Jean-Marie's idea and if I wanted to I could work with him. He was the manager of a community project in the suburbs, focusing on adolescents and their families. They were mostly North and Central African people.

He was putting together a group of sessional staff, in support of the full-time workers, whose role it would be to organise leisure activities and weekend outings. I became part of that group. Here my particular skills in the language stood me in good stead on the street, if disapproved of in their homes.

Letters from home told me of the birth of a niece; a sibling's illness; who had got a new job; and other neighbourhood tit-bits. I replied with reports of my experiences, living every moment, rattling along.

One weekend, the following spring, we stayed in a chalet in the picturesque Vogues, with six youths from the project, enjoying the last of the winter snow.

We had had a successful day tobogganing and after good food and wind-down activities we hit the sack. The shouting initially seemed to be in my dreams, but I woke with the light on in my room, looking into the eyes of a cat held upside down by its legs just above my face. Luc, a boy of about fourteen, was shouting angrily at me that I was useless to him, that I couldn't help him because I wasn't able to tell what was going on inside his head and that nobody would know only himself. Before anyone could react he hit the poor creature a chopping blow to the back of its neck and its tongue fell limp from its mouth. As droplets of blood began to form on the cat's nostrils, another boy, Abdul-Karim, the one we were supposed to be watching carefully over the weekend, took the cat, placed it on the floor and put his arms around Luc. I watched experienced staff calmly take the situation under control while I was taken to the kitchen for a hot sweet drink to calm my rattled nerves.

Luc was already under the supervision of the children's court; the judge had to be told. She sent him for psychiatric assessment. In writing about work in my next letter home, I conveniently left this incident out.

As I remember it, Luc was a turning point, another crossroads. The cat's tongue was the vision that returned, Luc's voice the sound, and above all that, Abdul-Karim's calm – he'd seen it all before. But I had found something of value and wanted to know more.

On his way to Germany, Ray visited me in Strasbourg. Over dinner he told me that he was leaving the priesthood. I responded by saying it was the honest thing to do, really. He said that his dilemma was that he felt unqualified to do anything else and he was thinking of going back to college to study psychology in Dublin, because some of his current qualifications were not recognised for employment purposes in Ireland. This focused my attention on a potential problem that I hadn't thought of. Ray asked me what I thought of *Dubliners*. 'I really enjoyed it,' I said, though I hadn't read it. That evening I rooted it out from a box on top of my wardrobe and began reading. When I finished 'Eveline', I stuck a photograph in the page and fell asleep.

I enjoyed the work I was doing; couldn't have been happier. Sometimes out of my depth, on unfamiliar ground, but that was the point. If I wanted to do this kind of work then formal training was required. So, documents were gathered and translated into French. References were sought. My application was sent and fingers were crossed. Doubts began to bother me. Emotional strings tightened when cards and telegrams arrived to wish me a happy twenty-first. Should I not be working with Irish children? If moving abroad was an attempt to find my own feet, had headway not been made? If it had to do with having an independence of thought, or with keeping my own head above the waterline in a society that would still resist contraception and divorce, and stigmatise our native minorities such as single parents and Travellers, would I not now better cope?

The letter of acceptance from the University of Strasbourg arrived, but my mind had already changed. For better or worse, I returned home, returned to an Ireland where the names of Joanne Hayes and Ann Lovett were as yet unknown, where a taoiseach voted against his own health minister's bill, and where an Irish solution to an Irish problem was still to be found.

I look at the faded colour photograph now. I think fondly of the man who held the camera in June 1971. I have no picture of Ray and never met him again after Strasbourg. Now, as before, I place the photograph of myself, my Honda CB 250 and the foyer de retraite *back among the pages of the book he had given me, a book that started another lifelong interest.*

III

'On my Manchester moon. . .'

from 'Landing in Manchester'
Rose Morris

JOHN MCAULIFFE

To and Fro

Past the Christie Hospital and around the back of Withington, through Fallowfield and then in and out along the Moss Side–Rusholme border and into Whitworth Park: in the decade I've lived in South Manchester, the streets on my cycle route have changed and changed again. The Golden Lion pub is a car park for the Christie Hospital staff; the White Lion is a Sainsbury's 'local'; the bank in Withington is closed down and up for sale. The old abandoned *Hans Knitwear* factory on Santiago Street has become an Islamic Centre where, each Friday, taxis queue or park on every corner; Rusholme's 'curry mile', its Pakistani and Bangladeshi restaurants, has been taken over by Iraqi and Syrian and Afghan and Libyan cafes and shisha bars – one night in October 2011 I couldn't get through at all when 30,000 Libyans gathered at the south end to celebrate the news about Gaddafi.

There are new Somali and Ethiopian restaurants on Claremont Road, and two of the last Irish bars in Rusholme, the Clarence and the Whitworth, have shut, the latter now a Christian café. The terraced houses around them bear the signs of this transient life. Stopped at the lights at the bottom of Platt Lane this morning, I could look up at a row of first-floor apartments with furniture backed against the windows, wardrobes and dressers blocking off the light; inside are the people who have travelled here from the four corners of the earth, as catalogued in Withington photographer Len Grant's Life Without Papers project. This is a city on the move, adapting to, and being adapted by, each new wave of displaced or opportunity-seeking emigrants that arrives on its Victorian streets.

Re-reading Liam Harte's wonderful anthology ahead of my workshops with the Irish writers' group at the Irish World Heritage Centre in Cheetham Hill in North Manchester, the kaleidoscope of Irish emigrant writing shook me again. Political and natural catastrophe, economic necessity, work opportunities, escape: the women and men who populate his pages made stories out of common experiences. It appears easy, sometimes, for historians and politicians to fold all those stories into a homogenous tale, but Liam's book makes their task a little harder. Yes, there are common themes and occasions, which are also the subjects of some of the stories and poems collected in this book: funerals, the ferry home, summer holidays and culture clashes. I recognise them as one grid I can place on the to-and-fro that I know, and that define part of the lives of neighbours on the street where I live. But it is easy to forget the varieties of Irish experience here, from the one-hundred-year-old Wexford woman who moved here to look after her brothers and outlived them, to the woman whose bus-driver father, a Dub, listened to Joe Duffy every day and, when his other daughter moved back to Wicklow, told me his grandson modelled his hurling skills on Ben O'Connor, the skilful Newtownshandrum speed merchant, my favourite hurler of the past twenty years. Such to and fro! Talking about Cork club hurling on a corner of the Wilmslow Road! (But then Charlie moved back to Dublin, while his daughter moved to Scotland. And Nell died not long after she got her birthday letter from the Queen.) It has often felt in Manchester as if I am living here *and* in an Irish elsewhere, although the days still arrive when it becomes clear that I live in one place only, whatever else the ambient noise in the air around this house and these streets might suggest.

When, as part of this project, we sat down to read our work to one another on Wednesday nights in the Centre, it was clear that we all had similar to-and-fro journeys and occasions and experiences in common. And the bomb. The Provisional IRA's attack in 1996, a 1500kg bomb left in the back of a van in the middle of town, a day everyone in the room remembered, when a version of Ireland settled itself very squarely in the city. Some had been downtown when it happened. One remembered the confusion as German and Russian fans arrived for the next day's Euro 96 semi-final at Old Trafford. At home in Kerry, that bombing had been almost by-the-way, taking place a week after Sergeant Jerry McCabe had been shot in Adare, County Limerick. But acres of downtown Manchester had to be demolished, 212 people were injured, and tour guides still stop at the one red pillar postbox which withstood the blast in the Corporation Street area. In the workshop room, looking out big windows at Cheetham Hill, as this moment suddenly seized hold of the conversation, it was clear, in relation to this and much else, that we all wrote very differently in relation to what it was we had in common. Although it might be argued that what we had in common most of all was the desire to set things down on paper, to write.

*

Manchester had always appeared to me as more of a music city than a literature one: the Hallé, where Irish composer George Osborne made notes on one of the last performances by his friend Frederic Chopin; the music hall in Stalybridge in east Manchester where 'It's a Long Way to Tipperary' was first performed; the streets where The Smiths and Oasis developed distinctively witty and wordy songs, and where flautist Michael McGoldrick played in Toss the Feathers and, one night, as soloist in a performance of Mícheál Ó Súilleabháin's *Oileán/Island* at a packed Manchester Cathedral.

In keeping with that, during my years in Manchester, it had been music that stirred up the feelings I associated with emigration, which often seemed to be simply an intense nostalgia for childhood: you will know tunes which have that effect. For me, Ger Wolfe singing his way awkwardly through 'The Curra Road' in a YouTube video by a user called 'thatssamhesgreat' that has since been taken down, or Christy Moore covering a Wally Page song, or The Pogues doing 'The Body of an American' – these songs, with their rivers and harbours and fields and family talk, are almost dangerously attractive. Listening to them felt like an indulgence, and could be overwhelming. I didn't know the places in those songs, I'd only ever listened to them here in Manchester, but why did it feel like they 'took me back'? When the songs were over, and I was back in the land of the living and thinking, I could see that they had *made* new spaces.

In Liam's book, as we looked for writers who generated that kind of space, we picked out a dozen of the pieces as starting points, among them Margaret McAloren's Silvertown hurly-burly, Alice Foley's Bolton waltz, the helpless power of John Healy's *The Grass Arena*, Yeats's sly memoir of his first days at school in England as the Irish boy. I wasn't sure there *were* many poems about Irish Manchester that could reach that pitch, but we began by looking at the powerful disturbance of Bernard O'Donoghue's 'Immaturities', about his 'City mother's' response to his father's death. We travelled from that devastating scene ('the noise / That greeted us was a mad cow roaring') to a catalogue for a show by his cousin, the artist Hughie O'Donoghue, who grew up in Wythenshawe, and its evocative memoir of Maine Road, where his father watched matches from the side of the pitch and where, every so often, a train ran between the sideline and the stand. Which led us to the image of a turnip-snedder in the same catalogue, an image which Seamus Heaney picked up for the first poem in his 2006 collection *District and Circle*, a terrific, bleak poem whose confidence in its own phrasing (from warlike 'breast-plate' and 'greaves' to the farmyard's 'seedling braird' and 'snedder') led us into conversations about the way writers have to trust that the tools they have will lever the world into their work. I hope that these writers' confidence in the facts of their experience, and their imaginative shaping of those facts into poems and stories, comes across clearly in this section of this anthology, itself a select pick from the work they turned in, surprising me and I hope themselves, with what came up. Each week, hearing new poems and stories for the first time, I was sure that more *new spaces* were being made

*

My idea of place, or changing places, was formed, is still formed, by my home town, Listowel, a North Kerry market town like many other towns, which has long had a literary double life. John B. Keane ran a pub on William Street and the fiction writer Bryan MacMahon, retired from school-teaching, could be seen walking the streets or sometimes leading a group of tourists around the town on

Mart Day, describing its beauties, occasionally in French or Irish. There was nothing extraordinary then about seeing John B. in plain view as he took his daily walk by the River Feale: it was a mysterious and educational task, though, to square the writing with the fact of his wry, rheumy presence around town. He and Bryan wrote, unsentimentally, about the town's hinterland of farming villages and about the positive impact of modernity on old hierarchies: wised-up insiders with a natural sympathy for the outsider, they were a Kerry introduction to the doubleness of writing *life*.

Some things became clearer after I moved away, such as the connection between place and language: now, driving along the Cork-Kerry border in Sliabh Luachra, I know I'm almost home when I see the signpost for O Rathaille's 'stick' (or school). O Rathaille, and Eoghan Rua Ó Súilleabháin, are emblematic figures, eighteenth-century Irish-language poets whose writing lives were split apart, and made, by the shift in power and shift in language. One thing writers do is find the right names for places as well as for feelings and ideas, and sometimes the writing must just confess its own inadequacy to this task. Places exceed us, the old names tell us, and any new definitions we might wish upon these towns we leave and, every so often, return to.

And, no more than Manchester, the town continues to be productively perplexing and constantly in flux. When I'm at home I walk Market Street, past John B.'s, now run by his son Billy, and into the redesigned town square where the terrific converted church, St John's, hosts theatre and music every week; I walk past the extended Listowel Arms Hotel, where Charles Stewart Parnell made his last public address, and under Listowel Castle, whose ruin is now attached to an interactive museum which documents and celebrates the work of John B., MacMahon and other writers from the area. I take a camera out for a walk along the Feale, unsurprised by its slow transformations, veering left along the gravel footpath, behind the new development of townhouses, then down past the Co-op pumping smoke into the Kerry skies, before ducking under the bridge on the Abbeyfeale side of town and walking up through the Cows' Lawn (once the town's commons, now a pitch-and-putt course with tennis courts and a community centre) to the 'Garden of Europe', whose unusual and complicated design sets plants and flowers from every (pre-2004) state in the EU around a bust of Schiller and a memorial to the Holocaust.

*

As the classes progressed, we continued digging around for material, both there and here, stretching to Vona Groarke's Manchester poems, Thomas Kinsella's brief childhood spell (during the Blitz) in Gorton, poems about emigration and return by Colette Bryce and Eavan Boland. At some point I made the connection between Eva Gore-Booth and the Booth Street I drove along on my way to the workshop, discovering that the Booth family fortune had subsidised the Sligo house which Yeats had visited as a child and where he had set his great poem, 'In Memory of Eva Gore-Booth and Con Markiewicz', in which it suddenly seems to occur to him that all of his effort and attention have not been able to preserve the culture and art he values, that it may all not have been worth the candle: 'Bid me strike a match, and blow', the poem ends. I discovered that Eva Gore-Booth had returned to Manchester and had had an inspiringly irregular life of her own here, involved in the suffragette movement, teaching as part of the university's outreach programme in Ancoats, and living with her partner Esther Roper in Heald Place in Rusholme, one of the terraced houses I cycled by each morning and evening. It was an irresistible set of stories, especially given my immersion in what increasingly looked like a secret Irish literature of the city.

The fact that Gore-Booth's feminism and educational work chimed with Liam's anthology only gave further impetus to writing which developed into 'Vague Urania', a poem which became part of the *Home, Alone* sequence of poems that Gallery Press published in *The Way In*, which appeared just as the workshop series was drawing to a close. That sequence, like the work collected here, moves backwards and forwards between Manchester and Ireland and borrows some elements from the Elizabethan poet Edmund Spenser, a migrant writer himself who wrote most of his work in North Cork, with occasional journeys back to England. Spenser is still identified with the dire colonial project in which he made his career (it was Yeats, brilliantly, who called him the first *state* poet), but it was easier to respond to his inventiveness and gorgeous rhythms as I re-read Liam's anthology and spent time working with writers who were making new poems and stories at the point where the sharp edges of national identity *could* do their most limiting and imagination-deadening work. Reading and writing together over a couple of months, it was clear how hard it is to escape such dividing and defining categories – the proper nouns of nation states – and to trust instead that the work could make its way without them in the vaguer, darkening and fast-moving currents we recognised in the places we write from.

Vague Urania

A terrace in Moss Side with Esther Roper
and, for cover, her brother, redbrick outreach and 'sex
is only an accident'. Join the union. Workers
knew her, who she was, and didn't care:
one of the Gore-Booths, who hears the 'dearer
waves of Breifni'. . . If she walks out Booth Street,
Lissadell's there: its western coast

is part of her position, but the town
is her arena, an outpost of the future.
She is her sister's keeper and guardian
of the acrobat, the gymnast,
barmaids, flower-seller and waitress, no, waiter,
writer, teaching poetry at the Round House
on Every Street, driving a coach-and-four

up a dry woodland path not just anyone can enter,
where a bust of Lenin and a portrait of Napoleon
settle down in a biggish house, in the ante-room,
like characters from her *World Pilgrim*
sharing a sick joke about what used to happen
in the garden, in the belvedere. Strike!
This wasn't the teddy bears' picnic.

And now? A semi in the suburbs lets the terrace. Digs,
through which strange life passes, 19,
20, 21; the former factory, *Hans Knit*,
is a mosque with tall weeds and a Friday crowd,
laced trainers and starlings on a redundant line.
Everyone around is mobile: rooms, services,
blow, change hands for half nothing, more or less.

On Heald Place junk and parcel, will
and codicil, pile up, 'not known at this address'.
Dreaming up a subject, knock the walls
about an iron bed on which nothing's built
and Urania is to be found. Free
and silent now as a hand reaching out for a waif,
'more, more,' its dream double as constant as life.

ROSE MORRIS

Landing in Manchester

Birch Lane bedsit.
Wallpaper peeling
from sloping ceilings
of an attic room.
A gurgling reaction
in the header tank
from a downstairs flush
brings battering pipe
and fading trickle.

A single light bulb
hangs on a dusty wire.
Bakelite switch dangles
above the bed.
A rusty gas ring coils
on a corner table.
Lingering odours
in curtain folds
and blankets.

First summer in a city,
in the heat of July.
A green grime-clad
skylight window
filters a ray of sunlight
to a threadbare carpet
rippled by floor boards
worn away by the feet
of my predecessors . . . fellow emigrants.

Background music
from a portable radio
permanently tuned
to Radio Éireann.
Saturday's sponsors
'Cakes by Gateau'

'The Kennedys of Castleross'
Walton's record shop
'If you feel like singing . . .'

I dwell on recent news
of the first moon landing.
Broken on piped radio
in the heat and fumes
of welded raincoats
in a Cheetham factory.
'One small step . . . One giant leap'
My new space, a first step
on my Manchester moon.

BRIDIE BREEN

Crossing Over

One moment here
One moment there
Dublin Manchester
Manchester Dublin
I lose track of where I am
momentarily I lose track of me.

Hustle bustle
Migratory nation
Holidaymakers
Children sense anticipation
Tired travellers
Occasional shrieks
Suitcased maniacs
wheel over toes.
Driven to be first in queue
Why does rush matter so much?

I look around to see
fellow wanderers
Wishful thought
not to be caught in
anything other than
moving through time
together.

No crashes
No turbulence
Just a smoothness
which glides through the sky
and lands me safely
Back from there to here
on the other side.

Drip Drip Drip Daddy

Childhood recall stands me
a pale, skinny-legged creature
in a white petticoat.
Awaiting a wash
in a scullery room, before bed.
The Belfast sink so deep
its base filled with
a thousand minute cracks.
Ice cold water
flowed to freeze a tender scalp.

The draining board creaked
as pestered digits
sought out scattered tools.
Stripy braces pinged
when you bent over too far,
I was more than amused.
A stretch across pursed lips
steeled by an intense stare.
You fiddled with copper piping
washer missed, vice gripped
both fingers instead, cursed
and muttered every synonym of *fool.*

A single forehead vein bulged
exerted and enraged
snaked a path amid perspired droplets,
hinged on bushy eyebrows
above a focused glare.
I place you, Daddy, centre stage,
drag you out laughing
from my Pandora's boxed-off
cobwebbed brain.
Thoughts wash over my sands of time
Solidified now by wiser eyes.

At seven years old,
a freshly communioned self,
I try to recollect it all.

Trudge through the dense mist of memory
to find the sweet softness
of her smile again.
The Angelus pause
for the decades of rosary at tea.
Magnificat recited at six o'clock by family
devotion to the purest
Mother of all Mothers
called a halt to the plumbing,
while the labourer knelt in prayer.

At a safe distance
out of arms reach
I stand shivering
to hover in the doorframe.
Two slender pipes stand anew,
you weave from side to side
to admire the work,
then turn to silently inspect me.
Hair strands sucked
in fretted consideration
I hide, for fear the light behind
flimsy *broderie anglaise* fabric
can trace my outline, too sheer.

Now, I flashback from time to time
when I run to tighten taps.
I choose to exculpate deeds in memoriam,
saged words of my mother philosopher,
mantras embedded so deep in my mind.
I still hear her voice instruct,
check carefully whether the good
characteristics outweigh the bad,
and remember
no one is perfect in this life.

Martha Ashwell

Sights and Sounds

The model village of Bessbrook, built from local granite, born of Quaker vision, lies close to Slieve Gullion Forest Park. Tourists come to see the old linen mill, Craigmore viaduct sweeping across the valley, the Yellow House at Derrymore, the derelict police station, now redundant. It's a place known for its troubles and for its industry. The gentle sounds of the sheep and the cows can still be heard in the soft green fields.

Yesterday, in Bessbrook, I heard two men talking over their pints.

For the love of Jesus, I said. Stop faffin' about you big lump, get out of your bed and get yer'self a job. Ach, he didn't like that. Called me an eejit, so he did. It had to be said, Jim, it had to be said. Dad, he said. What do you know? Sure, you'd buy a chocolate fireguard as soon as look at it. Always know better than we do, the young 'uns! Right, Jim, I'm away home for me tea.

Many years ago my father transplanted himself from Bessbrook to Manchester. A schism developed, a split, a painful division that remains open to the sky and raw like a cut to the bone. Manchester, his adopted city, boasts a cathedral, a neo-Gothic town hall and an impressive central library. The city was not unkind to my father but his body took some peculiar twists and turns in its attempt to survive as an immigrant in England.

Today, in Manchester, I overheard two women talking at the corner.

Jesus Christ, what do ye bloody want from me woman? Oh, stop your mitherin', I said to 'im. I'm that fed up with it, Teresa! D'you know, it's not worth the bother. As if it wasn't hard enough without the drinkin'. Know what you mean, Agnes, know what you mean. Honest to God, I can't take much more.

My defining colours are the green of the land and the blue of the sea. It is my heartstring pulls me to Ireland, as though it were a nerve or tendon sustaining my soul. It would be great if I could buy a home there so I could go over whenever I wanted and invite friends to join me in my search for the missing links of my childhood.

The little house my father left behind was where his family would remain. The Victorian house in Manchester would provide a bedsit, a place for him to live, sleep and eat, interspersed with outings to the pub to drown his sorrows.

The green fields and mountains of Bessbrook were far away from the industrial grime of prosperous Manchester. But this was where the work was. Here, among the grey streets and blackened buildings with the noise and bustle of trams and buses and trains. Work, the defining element of existence; nothing compares to its importance; everything pales into insignificance beside it.

The sun sets over the lake at Camlough. The birds fly in formation seeking a quiet spot for the night. Reeds swish and rise from the water, kissing the night sky. They are too weak to rely on; easily swayed, yet packed close together they cover the roofs of houses and seal them from torrential rain. How clever is nature? It provides us with everything we need. The village settles down to sleep. Doors are locked and cats put out.

The sun sets over Manchester. The birds fly in formation seeking a quiet spot for the night. The factories, office blocks, department stores and warehouses stand tall against the night sky. Doors are locked and cats are put out. But the city stays alive until dawn, alive unto another day.

DES FARRY

News from Faraway Places

It was late October 1962.

I remember catching the bus to school and asking the conductor Tads Bell for a return ticket. He said, 'Buy a single and spend the change on sweets at Wellworths. No point buying a return today. The way things are you might not have a home to come back to anyway.'

All the classroom doors on the paved passage along the main stone building were left open. Brother Mullins was patrolling about outside with an air gun. The teachers' raised desks at the top end of each room directly faced the doorways. Our classes, E1 and E2, had adjacent doorways and between them outside was a chair with a transistor radio switched on, just loud enough for the teacher and the first few rows to hear. It was tuned to BBC Northern Ireland and you could just make out the voice of Michael Baguley, the Northern Irish version of Richard Dimbleby.

Like Dimbleby, you would never get Michael on fun shows on TV or radio. You'd never see him eating yellowman at the Ould Lammas Fair at Ballycastle or trying to climb the greasy pole at the Clabby All-Ireland Donkey Derby. He was a straight news and current affairs man who only did serious stuff.

At the morning break there was a rumour that we were finishing at lunchtime. An unexpected half-day off was in prospect but how the morning dragged on. A first period of English literature with Nick Nicholson on *Twelfth Night*, its plot and sub-plot involving Malvolio.

Chriiiist! We hated Shakespeare with a passion!

It was during the first bit of a double period of French, when we were reading and translating aloud Balzac's *Le Curé de Tours*, that it happened.

'I've got him! I've finally got him!' shouted a triumphant Brother Mullins, appearing at the door holding a large rat by its tail. Something on the radio caught his ear as he dropped the rat and turned up the volume.

'The ships have all stopped at anchor and some are starting to turn back east. It looks like the start of the ending,' announced Michael Baguley.

A look of relief from the French teacher was soon replaced by his usual gloating expression.

'I think, boys, that the rumoured half-day off this afternoon will no longer take place,' he said.

KEVIN MCMAHON

First Television

21 October 1966

Excitement welled like an unseen spring,
That last day before the half-term break.
With skies dark and thick as coal sludge,
The rain – for the second day that week –
Had left us trapped in classrooms
Behind high, steamed and streaming windows.
I ached for the release of the evening bell.
Lessons ambled past my reverie,
Anticipating Bilko's antics,
Concocting Oxo-family tableaux,
A cocoon of laughter, where Michael Miles
Presided over 'Yes-No interludes'.

Unleashed by school's end we ran,
A yelping avalanche splitting the gloom.
A knot of women huddled sombre at the gate,
Heads scarfed against the rain, in quiet talk.
Blushing at my mother's long embrace,
And pulling at the hand that gripped my own –
With more than usual tightness –
I rattled out my plans, my hopes,
As she palmed the raindrops from her face.

It sat, intruding on the normal,
On splayed and spindly legs.
Chairs, newly shifted to strange places,
Shrank the little parlour.
Its unfamiliar light transformed
Our faces, pallid as we watched
A silent throng of mothers
Where the gates had been,
Heads scarfed against the rain.
They stood and stared at rooftops
Protruding from the spoil,
And waited for their children.

Limbo

The day Elvis died
I was home on holidays.
We scrambled over the bridge
To pick our way along the river
Until we got there.
A boundary-land, where parishes met
To shrug off their responsibilities.
Bee-laden air shrouded ground
Where the unbaptised lay
Unforgettably ignored.
I asked her the name of this place:
Srath na Leanbh – the Child Field.
I tested those syllables,
My mouth sullenly awkward.
She laughed at me.

She tested my old slender consonants
With the names of townlands,
Aughalánsín, Carrascehín,
But each betrayed my flat
And faithless tongue;
Coarsened by Manchester streets,
Blunted by fear and fist.
I knew that moment
That I was in a boundary-land
Caught between the tones
Of desire and necessity
And lost to both my worlds.

Annette Sills

Seesaw

The thought of touching it makes my tummy go round and round like a cement mixer. He asked me to do it last night but I got out of it when Stella knocked on to see if I wanted to play tap latch on The Twits at number seven. I know I'm going to have to do it at some point though. He is my Dad after all.

Me and Stella hate Mr and Mrs Finch. They're Hells Angels. He's got a long dirty beard with bits of last week's food in it and she's proper mardy. They've got a fat motorbike with a big Union Jack flying off the back and they've stopped us playing kerby anywhere in the street just because Stella smashed the ball against their door once. Dad hates them too. On our way back from the park on Sunday Mr Finch was getting on his bike.

'See your lot have been at it again,' he said as we passed. Dad ignored him, gripped my hand and marched ahead, swinging the rounders bat high in the air. Then as he was putting the key in our lock he said the 'c' word. I gasped and looked around but Finchy was revving up by then and it got swallowed up in the noise.

When we got inside Dad walloped the bat down at the bottom of the stairs. I was scared it would wake Mum up and there'd be another fight. When he was getting me a drink in the kitchen later I asked him what Finchy was on about. His face wasn't beetroot any more but it was all creased like his accordion.

'The IRA killed the Queen's cousin yesterday,' he said, pouring me some Tizer. 'And if you ask me they could do with killing a few more along with him.' He must have seen how gobsmacked I was because when he handed me the beaker he winked, gave me a pretend smile and said, 'But don't be telling anyone that I said that now, will you?'

Mum and Dad laughed and Mum said, 'Good likeness' when I showed them my library book with the pictures of The Twits. They smiled at each other and it made me feel warm and gooey inside like when I scoop the hot chocolate sauce from Nan's sponge pudding and drip it onto the end my tongue.

I was going to tell Stella about the unmentionable when we were in Robin Park after school today. We were playing on the seesaw, balancing on the metal ridge in the middle and trying to keep both sides in the air. I can't tell anyone though. My life would not be worth living if it got round at school. It's too rank to even put into words.

I fold the butties in the scrunched up foil and put them in his bag hanging behind the door, ready for tomorrow. Her white Adidas bag is there too and as I'm running my fingers over the 'Keep the Faith' badge on the front, I hear him coming downstairs. Crikey. I do not feel one bit warm and gooey inside now.

He comes into the kitchen, shuts the door, pulls up a stool and sits with his back to me facing the window. Then he places a Boots bag and a packet of darning needles on the worktop.

I turn round and force myself to look at it, nestled between his shoulder blades under the grey white of his vest, a volcano ready to erupt. I swallow and look out of the window. The sky above the roof of the terrace backing on to ours looks like it's on fire and is the same colour as the sunburn on Dad's shoulders.

'You're a good girl to do this for me,' he says without turning round. 'It's awful painful when it rubs against the sacks I've to hump around at work.'

'She should be doing it. Not me. I'm only little,' I want to reply. But I hold my tongue and say, 'It's OK, Dad' instead.

She should be making his butties and his tea every night too but that's not happening either. They haven't spoken for over a week. That's the way it goes in our house. Up and down all the time. The bad feeling builds and pumps up like a balloon, then it explodes and splat – all the nasty stuff comes shooting out.

I dive under the covers in my bed when it happens. I put my fingers in my ears and pray that when I come out I won't be in a broken home like Vicky Melling, whose Dad left her Mum for a redcoat from Butlins in Filey.

I might never go to Ireland again if Mum and Dad split up. No more night crossings and being blown up and down that windy deck with Dad and watching the black waves crashing down below. No more roller skating in the village with my New York cousins or driving Grandad's tractor or sliding down hay stacks. It'll be just be me and Mum and a flask on a day out in Rhyl.

She's in the living room now moving chairs around. Dad clears his throat and shifts in his seat. The minute he's out of the door she's in there doing her moves. She'll be warming up for later.

Nan said she's reliving her youth. We had one of our chats when I stayed over on Saturday. We were playing Cluedo on the coffee table in front of the gas fire and sharing a box of orange and lemon slices.

Nan is beautiful and kind. She's big-boned, wears maxi–dresses, loads of beads and orthopaedic shoes. She always lets me be Miss Scarlett and says things like, 'Live and let live' and 'Give peace a chance'. She lives with her best friend Josie. They're very close.

When I told her Mum had had been staying out again her bosom heaved with a sigh. 'She loves the bones of you, you do know that, don't you?' she said. 'But she was just a girl when she had you, barley eighteen, and now she's making up for those years of partying she missed out on.'

'But *Dad* doesn't go to all-nighters every Friday and Saturday night.'

'I know, pet. It's this Northern Soul thing. It's way out of hand. Half the kids in this town are Casino obsessed.'

I chewed on a lemon slice, a fat, jellied slug in my mouth, and I watched her take big gulps of G and T from a tumbler with yellow daisies painted on the side.

'Your Mam and Dad are very different,' she said. 'Your Dad's older and more set in his ways. He likes his own music and his books and that funny football he listens to. Nothing wrong with that. The Irish have their own culture. They like to do different things.'

She looked dreamily into the fire.

'Not one of them came to the wedding,' she said, as if she was talking to herself. 'Not one. I wouldn't mind but she wasn't even Protestant. She was never brought up with any religion. She was just a young girl who got into trouble.' Then she turned round and shook the dice.

'Your Mam's only out dancing, love. You love your Irish dancing too don't you? I heard your Dad telling someone in town the other day about you being picked for the regionals. He's ever so proud.'

I looked down and moved Professor Plum four spaces for her. I felt bad. I like going to the feises and seeing my friends and everything but these days I prefer dancing round the living room with Mum to Frankie Wilson and 'Do I Love You'.

Sometimes I feel like I'm straddling two different worlds, like I'm on that seesaw in Robin Park, moving from one side to the other. But the way I see it, I come from both Ireland and England and I don't like it when Stella asks me which I like best because I love them both the same. I'm like that funny-looking plant I saw in Nan's mate Derek's conservatory once. It had two long straggly roots, each one in a different pot.

When I looked up Nan was gazing at me.

'It'll sort itself out,' she said, leaning over and squeezing my hand.

That made me want to cry and I wondered if I should tell her about the car crash dreams but I decided not to in case I got Mum in even more trouble. When she got in on Sunday morning I overheard Dad telling her she was a disgrace and she shouldn't be out speeding at her age. She must be doing it in someone else's car though because I when I get out of bed and check, ours is always parked outside. Anyway, now I have nightmares about her dying in a car accident. As if I've not got enough to worry about, what with the divorce, the unmentionable and Finchy coming after Dad because he thinks he's in the IRA.

Oh, I love this one. It's 'There's a Ghost in my House'. I know all the words and Mum taught me where to clap. I'd love to be in there with her now practising my back flips.

Dad pulls off his vest.

'Are you ready, sweetheart?'

My tummy does a massive somersault like it did when we dropped down on the Big Dipper in Blackpool. I fumble with the pack of darning needles and take out the biggest. I concentrate on the words of the song to distract myself. It's about a man whose wife runs off and leaves him and there's one line that goes, 'I just keep hearing your footsteps on the stairs, when I know there's no-one there.'

It's proper sad.

I turn to face it, holding the needle tight between forefinger and thumb. It stares back at me with its white cyclops eye.

'Keep still Dad,' I say, trying to contain the quiver in my voice. 'It'll be all over in a jiffy and you won't feel a thing.'

'Right you are soldier,' he replies and I'm wondering if it's too late to fetch my swimming goggles when I hear the creak of the door handle behind me.

'What's going on?'

Mum is standing in the doorway with her hands on her hips, taking in the scene. She's in her going-out clothes: red circle skirt, royals, ankle socks and buttoned-up blue polo shirt. She looks down at the floor, a bit lost, her hair flopping down over her eyes. We curled it together earlier with the heated rollers. She's got turquoise glitter on her eyelids. Stella thinks she looks like Jaclyn Smith and Derek goes bright red and fidgets with his specs a lot whenever Mum comes round to his house with me and with Nan.

She steps towards me and I can smell Harmony hairspray and Anais Anais.

'Give me that,' she sighs, grabbing my wrist. I pull back at first, thinking she might hurt Dad, but I hand her the needle, then turn away and pretend I'm looking for something in the cupboard. Dad says something I can't make out and she laughs. Then I hear a sharp intake of breath and a low moan.

'Pass me a clean dishcloth from the drawer, pet,' she says. I keep my face turned away as I hand it over, as there are still dying animal noises coming from Dad. 'Nearly done,' she says in a sing-song voice.

From the corner of my eye I see her small hand rummaging in the Boots bag and the bloodied cloth next to it.

When I finally look, the wound is hidden by a neat square of gauze framed by strips of elastoplast, like a window with net curtains. She presses down on the plasters to secure them, then places her hand gently on Dad's shoulder.

Without turning round he places his hand on top of hers and for a few seconds I am back in the park on the metal ridge on the seesaw, my arms outstretched, balancing, neither up nor down, my two worlds joined in one.

ANN MARIE TOWEY

Mayo Votes

My mother had never wanted to return to Ireland. She could only remember the gruelling life of work on a farm and she refused even to go with us on the only occasion we visited as children. My father, who had run away to England at the age of sixteen, was obsessively nostalgic about Cloonlarin, the place of his birth. He knew which field his brother planted every year, the nature of the crop, the number of cattle and how the harvesting and turf-cutting fared. So, when my cousin visited us in Manchester in 1982, and was questioned closely, it was easy for my father to catch her out in knowing precisely where the carrots had been sown. At the time, I had nothing else to do so I decided to return with Ann and spend a week reconnecting with my Irish roots. At the time, I suppose she represented a new, modern Ireland and I was interested to see whether my mother's view of a country of deprivation would prevail over my father's romantic perception of his homeland.

We caught the Walls coach in Fallowfield which would drop us off in Charlestown. That summer, Ireland was abuzz with talk of its referendum on abortion, which was still over a year away. The people were deciding. On Sunday, we went to mass in Tubbercurry. It was a warm, drowsy summer's morning and the church was heaving. Large families of freckle-faced children were stuffed into each pew. The sunshine streamed through the stained glass windows, dappling rainbow colours over the modern, Celtic-hut-design interior. The mass began and the rather frail elderly priest murmured the opening prayers. We then settled down to hear his homily.

He began so softly. I was lulled. Reminding his parishioners of the momentous decision the country was making, he outlined Catholic teaching on the issue. Everybody seemed to be listening, with heads meekly bowed and in full agreement.

As he warmed to his theme, I jolted with surprise. What was he saying now? What was he talking about? Was I really hearing this?

'Now, ye all know, during the war there was a great shortage of rubber, but there was never any shortage of rubber to make them aul condems.'

Yes, condems.

I reeled.

It is now hard to think back to a time of innocence and, yes, squeamishness, but this was an age before the threat of the AIDS epidemic, before those public awareness broadcasts with great tombstones rolling through a darkened, underwater nuclear disaster zone with that deep, sinister Armageddon voice of doom warning everyone against unprotected sex.

'Condoms' was a word I had never heard uttered in polite society and I had certainly never imagined I would hear it – pronounced like that – from the pulpit.

I looked round the church. Not one person – man, woman or child – had reacted in any way. They still had their heads meekly bowed. I couldn't even catch anyone's eye.

By this time, the priest was thundering his message across.

'Now I know ye all have your democratic rights, but I am *ordering* you, yes *ordering* you, as your parish priest to vote 'no' in this referendum. Now let us all rise to say the Creed.'

Mass finished and on the way out I tackled my cousin about all we had heard. It was unimaginable for a priest in England to deliver such a homily, I assured her.

'Fwat? Fwat?' she asked, clearly mystified. 'What did he say? Ah, sure, I never listen to them.'

I repeated all I had heard. She doubled up with mirth.

We crossed the road and went into Cawley's Hotel and sat up at the bar. Ann ordered a round of drinks and then made me repeat to the landlord what I had heard. Soon, the whole bar was rocking with laughter. I couldn't work out whether they were amused by my quaint reaction to what I had heard or whether this was the first time any of the priest's parishioners were aware of his sermons.

PATRICK SLEVIN

The Woman in Our Prayers

We travelled in black suits and they kept the coffin open.
She hadn't been gone for three days.
The rosary-filled rooms were empty without her.
It had been coming for at least a year.

The set-dancing ladies stood a guard of honour
All the way down the narrow front path.
She was hard to carry in the dark of November.
Her grandchild was kept in the house.

The first time they'd met, had been her last smile.
A single light in the road.
But they heard us for miles as we followed the hearse,
The only car moving through town.

Remember the summers with strange-coloured money,
Different collectors at Mass.
You threw sticky weed on me and laughed as you ran.
You hadn't been tired from work.

She walked down this way every dark Sunday evening
Before they got the phone.
'She'll be at the neighbours,' you'd say and hang on for ten minutes,
Then you'd sit on the stairs for an hour.

You'd come back with your accent and that look in your eyes
And say there's no news at all.
'The place is still there and she was asking about you.
Remember that woman in your prayers.'

She'd sent over newspapers wrapped in a brown band.
You dared us to touch them, 'just once'.
You hid away in full view, for weeks in the front room,
Till the ink ran out of your eyes.

There's a shop down in Burnage that gets them in every weekend
If the weather's good for the boat.
I can run down and get one, it's no distance from Stockport.
It'll be different to get them on time.

'He's from England,' someone pointed as we carried her in,
To the church full of the town.
Condolence was whispered by everyone to the front row.
You shook hands with three hundred hands.

Kathleen Handrick

Maggie

Maggie wearily dropped her bag on to her desk. It was a real burden today. She had slept badly, or rather Frank had slept badly, and long after he settled after his cramp she had lain awake, thinking. In the past, she had used such times to pray. Of course, then she would be praying that one or other of the children would be safe – at a nightclub, at university, backpacking or enjoying some other worrying activity – and Frank would be steadily sleeping beside her, blissfully unaware of her anxieties. Now, the children were away and settled and it was herself and Frank who needed her prayers. Somehow, though, that was becoming an increasingly difficult task.

Frank had never had an outgoing personality; he wasn't a bit like the Irish boys she'd met when she first settled in Manchester. The craic was great with that crowd, dancing every weekend at the clubs, and she was as surprised as anyone when she agreed to go on a date with Frank. She was a primary school teacher and he was working on a refurbishment in the school. There was something so steady about him. She liked his manners and his dry sense of humour and his family were great with her, especially his dad. She used to love to listen to his stories of the industrial town – such a contrast to her rural upbringing. There was always music in the house, from musicals to opera, and although they weren't keen on showbands, they did enjoy singing along to the Clancy Brothers. Frank's family weren't a bit bothered about her religious faith; they had none really, so it didn't matter. Her mother, however, was quite distressed when Maggie told her of her intended engagement to Frank. Even after their marriage, it took a few years for him to be fully accepted but by the time the children came along, Frank's decency and quiet ways were boasted of back home.

Since his redundancy, though, Frank had changed, become withdrawn, almost silent. He had received a good settlement so it wasn't the loss of an income. It was that he felt worthless. Too much time on his hands, he complained. He felt rejected and had become a very different kind of man. She, though, seemed to have too little time – planning, paperwork, meetings and then running the home. She was retiring in the summer and the plans and hopes that they had previously shared seemed impossible now. She was dreading all that free time with him.

Thank God for the Easter break, I'm tired out, she thought. Molly often thanked God like this: that Frank had managed a bit of a walk today, that Eddie had phoned at last, that Catherine was still enjoying the job. It was just a habit of old. 'Buíochas le Dia'. She could hear her mother's response during those long

Friday evening telephone conversations when Maggie would be filling her in on the family's latest news: Frank's promotions, Eddie's latest football trophies, Catherine's exam successes, she, herself, still working at the same school, still teaching the little ones.

Her mother meant it though; she was great at the praying. As soon as the phone was put down, she knew Mammy would be there with her rosary and pleading to every saint she knew for any help needed in the family. It was all so normal and positive then. I wish you were here now, Mammy, and your friend St Jude! Nowadays it's more 'where are you God?' she mused.

She began to unpack her bag and stood her files of planning, observations and records on the shelf behind the desk. They were up to date and, more importantly, out of the way now for the holidays, thank G—. She stopped the thought abruptly. Lastly, she pulled out a plastic storage box. Inside could be seen the blurred outline of biscuit-coloured blocks. They were flapjacks she had made last evening as a treat for the children on this last day of term. Maggie prepared toast for them most mornings and after registration they would sit in a circle on the carpet sharing the bread.

Several children, she knew, wouldn't have eaten a breakfast and this ritual was designed to feed them and also calm the class and set them up for the day. Her thoughts turned to Callum's review last evening. The family worker seemed to be better than the last one. He understands the difficulties – strong support is needed. I hope mum listens this time, it must be her last chance. There's got to be an improvement for Callum's sake. He was such a concern to Maggie, one of the several who had unhappy or hectic homes and this bit of attention really made a difference to his behaviour.

At the latest development meeting the advisor, who couldn't have been much older than Catherine, had pointed out that 'love wasn't enough for these kinds of children', they needed skills. She had continued to list the outside influences which could affect their learning: dysfunctional families, economic migrants, refugees and so on. Maggie was so irritated but kept quiet. Without love, they are nothing, and they're doing fine with me, thank you!

Today was Spy Wednesday and after registration she was going to explain the meaning of Good Friday to the children. After all the negativities about the Church in the last few years, Maggie thought that the clergy seemed to have gone back to the old authoritarian practices but without the love or the humanity. Something had died, somehow. It had in her at least. Father Earnshaw was one of this new breed of priests. He had said that teaching the Resurrection must be left until after Easter. He liked things done in the proper order. But Maggie knew that she would finish the whole story today. They were only five years old after all and it would be too late after the holiday. It would mean nothing then. They would only remember the Easter eggs they would get at home time.

The children came into class, eager to share the smallest bit of news with her. Those who had none made it up, it didn't matter. She was a willing and trusted listener. She began to call the register: Callum, Caitlin, Conner, Liam, Neve, Sheavon. A shared heritage perhaps? No, just the latest trends. What did it matter? Sure they have all kinds of names nowadays.

She thought about her own schooldays, her friends all with holy names. When she first began teaching it was all so much easier. Everyone went to church, everyone knew the saints and stories, everyone believed. But now . . . She missed mass herself sometimes, when she was tired or shopping or had another moment of unbelief. It was becoming so regular. What is happening to me? she wondered. What would her mother think?

After the shared feast, she took the figure of the crucified Christ down from the wall ready for the lesson. At Christmas, the children had walked the long distance to the church for their first class visit. Only Blessing, Zuzanna and Liam had been before with their families. The visit was a resounding success. They could have been in a palace or a castle. The vaulted ceiling, the stained glass windows, the statues – all fascinated and enthralled the children and they sang a lullaby to the baby Jesus in the crib before they left. Now, just a few weeks later, Maggie pondered, I have to tell them that He had died!

Using her experience and ability as a story teller, she explained the happenings of Holy Week. The children waved their paper palms as they shouted 'Hosanna' at Jesus's joyful entry into Jerusalem. They sat rapt at her feet as they experienced the waiting, the promises and the fear of those few days. Using simple language – love, good, unkind, frightened – they became aware of the events. She finished the story quietly and allowed them their thoughts.

'Aw, that's a dead sad story, i'nt it Miss!' She looked down at the child sitting at her feet, his eyes pooled with tears. For a moment she hesitated and then took a deep breath and composed herself. She leaned down and slipped him a tissue.

'Yes it is Callum, it's really sad. But it's not the end. After playtime, I'll tell you the next part and do you know, we will feel so much better. Just you wait and see! It will give us such hope and we must always hold on to that.'

Going Home

There was nothing for them there.

That spit of land breaking away
into the ocean – no power
to stop the flow –
The waves from Blacksod.

Hope-filled they looked to Holyoke.
But you, you hesitated, perhaps
one more season howking tatties
and then return.

Yet still there was nothing for you there.
The spring of expectation passed.
And the seasons turned to years
and the years grew to decades.

Did you dwell on that place,
longing for a misty, distant image?
Or were your memories drowned,
too painful to recall?

That gentle, highland bride,
your comfort, your scribe.
Lovingly, she eased the pain.
Paper bridges between you and them.

Alone again, in your sorrow, your loss,
they pleaded, you yielded.

Was there anything familiar?
Heart crushing, eyes searching
the bay, the fields, the banks, the shore.
The hair, the eyes, the chin.
Awkward gripping of hands.
Two brothers – two strangers.

You turned away, yearning for the city.
The close, the neighbours, the banter – the peace.

'There's nothing for me here.'

MARY WALSH

The Yellow Bowl

Waking up with a pulsating thumb, she asked herself why she had not simply thrown out the jam jar of old nails that had been lying in the tool box for years, untouched. Why did I struggle with the rusty lid? she wondered. Now this thumb is a bulging mess and the plaster stuck rigid with a day-old seepage of blood. Can't think of taking it off now. Too many things to do. Just cover it up. What the eye doesn't see the heart doesn't grieve.

Looking out into the garden, she could not believe the damage the rain and wind had done to the tomato plants in the night. 'They're banjaxed,' she said, laughing at how easily the word came into her mind. But some plants could be saved, she thought. With a prop or two they would be fine when time was found tomorrow. But when will I have the time tomorrow? And look, the flowers have taken a battering! But there was no one there to sympathise. Anyway, she mused, in a couple of months the garden will be no concern of mine, rain or no rain. 'Come on. To the work in hand!' she chided herself, moving back into the room. Get rid of anything that is not going to be useful. Remember, moving is painful. No time for sentiment.

She moved towards the stairs, catching in her glance the yellow bowl with the dark purple tulip embossed on the outside. A relic of the past, she thought. It had been handed down by her grandmother who had taken it from her home in Derry to Newry, where she had come to be married in 1881. Only recently had it been put back on the hall table, now that the children had grown up enough to stop the urge to throw each other around. Oh those happy days! But it will have to go. 'No handy little recesses or shelves in the flat,' she said aloud in the silence, aware of the increasing, echoing emptiness. Noise! Any kind of gentle noise is better than this vacant silence. Music, as Jim was fond of saying, has charms to soothe a savage breast.

She put on a Rachmaninoff CD, the one that was the screen music for *Brief Encounter*, and as it started she eased herself down on the bottom steps with the yellow bowl on her knee. She hummed along with the music and at the same time recalled that visit to Ukraine and the afternoon she had spent in Chekhov's house, where years earlier in his beautiful drawing room Rachmaninoff had played the piano. There was a photograph of the occasion hanging on the wall above, she remembered. Still humming to herself, she picked up the bowl and made her way upstairs to the spare room that had become the not-decided-yet room, thinking as she went that nobody tells you how awful it is to be leaving a house that you have lived in for forty years.

Slightly out of breath, she pushed the door open and put the bowl down on the rickety table. It swayed dangerously before accommodating the heavy weight. It has been like that since we moved in all those years ago, she remembered, for Jim wasn't a handyman. She had known that from the start. Pulling the old wicker chair near, she sat down again and recalled the sunny summer afternoon when they were out for a walk, proudly pushing their new pram. At the end of the road, old John, busy in his garage, came out to see their tiny baby. He peeped in, made some clicking noises and said, 'What a pity they have to grow up!' and then went on to show them the window frame he had made. Out of earshot, and in an effort to encourage Jim to do something practical in the house, she said, 'Look! Isn't he clever? He's made that lovely window frame all on his own.' She knew she had lost when he replied, 'Ah! But I bet he can't play the piano!' Anyway, mending old tables wasn't that important when there were four children to bring up. Oh, those early years when they were all tumbling up went so fast that they were teenagers before she could draw breath.

Easing herself up out of the wicker chair, she moved forward and almost fell over the box of old travel guides. When she had steadied herself she wondered, as she had many times, why she hoarded these things. Well, there will be no place for them where I am going, she decided. But the pull of the past was strong, too strong. She sat down again. With the fingernails of her useful hand she flicked up guides to Paris, to Cuba and several to Ireland, where for fifteen years they all went for the summer holidays. She lived again the excitement when they arrived, the welcome, the visits to places the children knew only through stories, the music and singing and the river running down behind the church where all the cousins spent most of their days.

Must get on with this work, she chided herself but she couldn't, for at her feet, lying face up in the box, she recognised the guide to Venice. 'Venice,' she whispered, and 'Venice' again. She turned it over and there on the cover was the picture of a handsome gondolier, dressed as she remembered in black and white, a straw hat with a red ribbon falling down his back, taking a group of smiling people across the water towards St Mark's Square in the distance. That holiday was special not only because of Venice; the children had presented it to them as a twenty-fifth wedding anniversary gift. It was the best holiday they ever had. Just the two of us, she remembered. And still in the drawer are the photographs of us both by the water just below the Rialto Bridge, where that beautiful young girl standing nearby was calling up and waving to a young man on the bridge. As she waved and called again and again, the shining bead bracelet on her arm rolled up and down, glistening in the sun. They continued waving and calling to each other in Italian, then suddenly he disappeared into the crowd. For a moment I thought of Romeo and Juliet, she remembered, and laughed to herself.

And those other photographs of Jim and herself in a gondola moving along the Grand Canal, and pictures of those beautiful churches, doors wide open, welcoming the world in to see some of Italy's famous paintings. Then in the evenings escaping from the crowds to enjoy lovely food and sometimes too much red wine in a small restaurant they had found by chance, far from the tourists and their cameras. How magical it all had been, she sighed, and promised herself that one evening she would sit down and go through all those photographs. But what an emotional evening that will be! Jim is not here. No one to say, 'And do you remember going on the boat to the islands, Murano and its beautiful glass and Burano where every house is painted a different colour? And the sun shone every day!' She wished for a moment that she had not opened the box, yet without thinking she found herself putting the Venice guide on the table beside the yellow bowl.

Dusting cloth ready, she reached out towards the table again but a great rush of nostalgia overwhelmed her. She saw the bowl when its home was out there on the landing window sill and had become a receptacle for hair slides, clips and bits and bobs of teenage years. Any small thing that was lost was likely to be found in the yellow bowl, and whatever was fished out was encased in hairs and dusty fluff. She turned it upside down. There was nothing there but some old train tickets from Leeds to Manchester that her son, in too much of a hurry to find the waste paper basket, had dropped in on his way downstairs the day he was leaving to start his year abroad.

She lifted the bowl off the table and held it close, as if it was one of her children, and said in the silence, 'Can't leave you behind. You could tell the story of our generations. Anyway, what's the matter with sentiment? What would I do without it now?' And she carried the bowl safely into the definitely-taking-with-me room. Then, biting her lip, she braced herself for the struggle with the sticking plaster.

ALRENE HUGHES

Manchester Skies

Early morning
The boat train rattles into Exchange Station.
Outside, gun-metal clouds
Lie low over blackened buildings.
Fine drizzle coats our clothes, faces, hair.

Midday
Miles Platting, straight off the street, two up two down
A stiff breeze reveals snatches of pale sky and
Shafts of sunlight illuminate
Years of dirt and grime.

Afternoon
Pans of scalding water, carbolic fumes
We scrub paintwork, windows, floors.
Net curtains flap on the line beneath
A tiny blue rectangle stretched over the yard.

Midnight
Half-light, a city sky
Devoid of darkness, moon and stars
Only the eerie glow of orange street lights
And the sweeping beams of cars.

Morning
We ride a bus to the end of the line
In search of the horizon
And find our sky – complete, huge, welcoming.
We fill our lungs with sweet clean air
And let our sore hearts – soar.

Soda Bread

Visiting relatives brought presents
Floury farls of soda bread
Twisted in tissue paper
A taste of home.

We'd devour them
Hungry for comfort
Knowing they wouldn't keep.
Left a day
They'd turn green
Tainted in the English air.

There's soda bread in Tesco's now.
I never buy it.

Scattering

You can google *diaspora*
See it defined in all its randomness
A throwing away. From the Greek words
Dia, across and *spora*, scattered.

I've never felt scattered
My planting across the sea
Was no act of careless casting
Of caution to the wind.

Easily transplanted to foreign soil
Anchored with strong roots
Heritage is in the bone
'They change their skies, but not their souls
Who cross the sea.'